Ready for
PET

D0784985

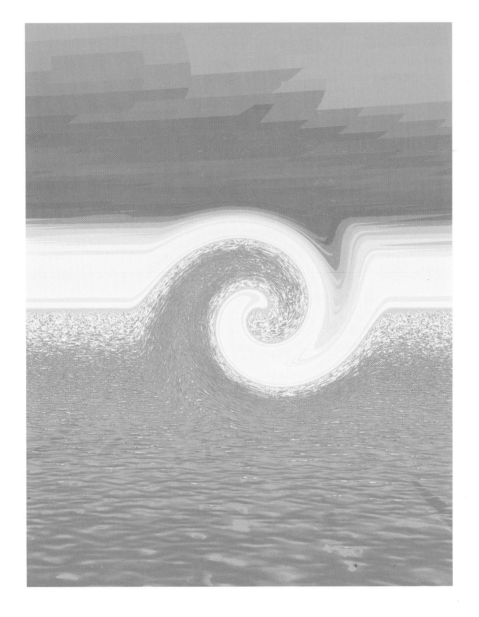

Nick Kenny   Anne Kelly

MACMILLAN
HEINEMANN
English Language Teaching

Macmillan Education
Between Towns Road, Oxford OX4 3PP
A division of Macmillan Publishers Limited
Companies and representatives throughout the world

ISBN   0 333 93393 1 (without Key)
        0 333 93392 3 (with Key)

Designed by Jim Evoy
Illustrated by Mike Atkinson and David Smith
Cover idea by Xen Media Ltd

The authors would like to thank Barbara Lewis in Pescara, Italy, for
her help with this book.

The publishers would like to thank the following consultants and
teachers for piloting and reviewing this book: Andy Hannaford,
Anthony Matthews, Barbara Lewis, Gail Butler, Mabel Turner and
Sarah Ellis.

The authors and publishers would like to thank the following for
permission to reproduce copyright material: University of
Cambridge Local Examinations Syndicate – EFL for the answer
sheets on pp.92–3.

LONDON METRO, for 'New Boy at University is Just Six', published
in Metro, 16 February 2000.

TIME OUT, for 'A Brood Awakening', published in Time Out No.
1563, 2-9 August 2000.

The authors and publishers would like to thank the following for
permission to reproduce their photographs: Sue Baker © MHELT
p18(br); Corbis pp21, 27, Corbis / Stephanie Colasanti 51, Corbis /
Michael Dunn 25(tr), Corbis / David Giles 25(tl), Corbis / Philip Gould
47(m), Corbis / Robert Holmes 38, Corbis / David Turnley 47(b), Corbis
/ Wartenberg 28, Corbis / Wartenberg 60, Corbis / David Wells 63(m);
Haddon Davies © MHELT pp8 (tmr), 16 (3, 4), 54(5); English Heritage
Photo Library p31; Eye Ubiquitous pp91(b), Eye Ubiquitous / Tim
Hawkins 48(m), Eye Ubiquitous / Craig Hutchins pp39, Eye
Ubiquitous / Craig Hutchins 41(b), Eye Ubiquitous / Craig Hutchins
48(ml), Eye Ubiquitous / Julia Waterlow 48(mr); Chris Honeywell ©
MHELT p18(mr); Image Bank pp43, 78(t), 91; MHELT pp8 (l, ml, m, r),
16 (1, 4, 5), 54(1, 2, 3, 4), 56 (2, 3, 4); Photodisc pp56 (1, 2);Pictor
p63(b); Stone pp19, 33, 41(t), 78(b), 42; Sunday Times (Funday Times)
p44; Telegraph Colour Library pp6, 12(tr); John Walmsley p12(tl).

Printed and bound in Spain by
Mateu Cromo

2005 2004   2003 2002
10 9   8   7   6   5   4   3   2

Contents

Introduction

Ready for PET is for students of English who are preparing to take the University of Cambridge Preliminary English Test (PET). *Ready for PET* will get you ready for this test in three important ways. First, it will give you practice in doing the kinds of exercises you will do in the test. Then, it will give you advice on how you can do your best in these exercises. Finally, it will help you learn the vocabulary you need to do the writing and speaking exercises fluently. In this way, you can feel confident about your English when you do the test.

You can use *Ready for PET* in your English class with your teacher, or you can use it to get ready for the test by yourself.

What is the Preliminary English Test (PET)?
The University of Cambridge has tests for students of English at five different levels, from beginners to very advanced students.
PET is at level 2 and is for lower intermediate students. PET tests your reading, writing, listening and speaking. You get 25% of the total marks for the test for each of these four skills. There are three different papers.

Paper 1 is Reading and Writing and takes 1 hour and 30 minutes. In this paper, there are five reading parts and three writing parts. In the reading part of the paper, you have to read some texts and answer some questions on each one. For these questions, you answer by choosing A, B, C, or D. In the writing part of the paper, you have to do a short grammar exercise, fill in a form and then write a letter. This is a summary of the Reading and Writing paper:

Paper 1: Reading and Writing (1 hour 30 minutes)			
	Type of text	Type of question	Number of questions and marks
Reading			
Part 1	five signs or notices	reading comprehension: multiple choice	5
Part 2	eight short texts	reading comprehension: matching	5
Part 3	one text	reading comprehension: correct/not correct	10
Part 4	one text	reading comprehension: multiple choice	5
Part 5	one text	vocabulary and grammar: multiple choice	10
Writing			
Part 1		grammar	5
Part 2		filling in a form	10
Part 3		writing a letter	10

Paper 2 is Listening and takes about 30 minutes. There are four parts to the paper. You have to listen to a recording and answer some questions. For the questions for three parts, you answer by choosing A, B, C, or D, and for one part you write down a few words or numbers. You hear each part of the recording twice. This is a summary of the Listening paper:

Paper 2: Listening (approximately 30 minutes)			
	Type of text	Type of question	Number of questions and marks
Part 1	seven short recordings (one or two people speaking)	multiple choice pictures	7
Part 2	one person speaking	multiple choice	6
Part 3	one person speaking	writing down words	6
Part 4	two people speaking	correct/not correct	6

Paper 3 is Speaking and takes 10–12 minutes. There are four parts to the paper. You do the Speaking test with another student. In the Speaking test, you and your partner talk to an examiner and to each other, while another examiner listens to you. The examiner will ask you some questions and give you some instructions about what you should talk about. In two parts, you have some pictures to talk about. This is a summary of the Speaking paper:

Paper 3: Speaking (10–12 minutes)	
Part 1	You and your partner ask and answer questions about yourselves.
Part 2	You and your partner look at some pictures showing a situation and talk about it together.
Part 3	You and your partner take it in turns to describe a photograph each.
Part 4	You and your partner have a conversation about the subject (eg holidays) of your photos.

You will find more detailed information about each part of all three papers in the different lessons of *Ready for PET*.

How Ready for PET is organized

There are ten units in *Ready for PET* and each unit has two lessons. In each unit, you will find exercises to practise the reading, writing, listening and speaking skills, and the vocabulary and grammar you will need in PET. In each lesson of Units 1–8, there is detailed information and advice about one particular part of the test, and in Units 9–10 you can revise all the advice that has gone before. Throughout the book there are **Get ready** boxes containing clear, helpful exam tips.

At the end of the book there are two PET practice tests. When you do these, you will experience what it is like taking the real test. You will see how much time you have to do each question and you will find out which parts of the test you need to practise more.

When you've worked through *Ready for PET*, you'll know what to expect in every part of the test, and you'll have the language you need to do the test well.

For students studying alone

If you are preparing for PET without a teacher, *Ready for PET* will help you. You should use *Ready for PET* at the same time as your general English coursebook. Your coursebook will develop your knowledge of English, and *Ready for PET* will give you the special practice you need for the test exercises.

There is a special 'with key' edition of *Ready for PET* which has a key to exercises and tapescripts of the listening texts at the back. When you have finished each exercise, check your answers with the key. Don't look at the key until you have done each exercise. If necessary, you can use a dictionary to help you with unknown words, but always try to guess the meaning of words first. You should also see if you can answer the questions without knowing the difficult words.

The texts of the listening exercises are on cassette. In the PET Listening test, you hear each listening text twice, so when you are practising with these exercises, rewind the tape and listen again before checking your answers. If you don't understand something you can look at the tapescript, but never do this until you have listened to the tape twice.

There are many writing exercises in *Ready for PET*. It's useful if you can ask a teacher to correct these for you, but it doesn't matter if this isn't possible. Just doing the writing is good practice. Always make sure you follow the instructions exactly and check your own work carefully.

There are also many speaking exercises in the book. It's difficult to do speaking exercises if you're studying alone, but it's important that you get speaking practice. Remember, 25% of the marks for the whole of PET are for the Speaking test, so if possible, do the speaking exercises with another student. If you can't do this, do the exercises by yourself, speaking into a cassette recorder. Then listen to yourself speaking and think of ways in which you could do the exercise better. Don't worry about making mistakes, but try to express your ideas clearly.

On pages 66–91, there are two practice tests. You should try to do at least one of these like a real test. Only take the amount of time allowed for the test, and do it without any dictionary or notes to help you.

Before you start, decide how many hours a week you can spend studying with *Ready for PET* and keep to this decision. It is better to study regularly for short periods than to try and do everything just before the day of the test.

The PET preparation diary on the opposite page will help you to organize your study. Fill in the date you start your PET preparation at the top, and the date you will take PET at the bottom. Then work out how many days or weeks you have to complete each unit of this book. When you have completed a unit, write the date in the space provided, and decide how well you have done in the different practice exercises in that unit (self-assessment). In the 'Study notes' section you can write anything which will help you. For example, you may want to make a note of some exercises you want to look at again, or some exercises which you haven't had time to do and plan to work on later. You should organize your study in the way which best suits you in the time you have available before you take PET.

Unit	Study notes	Self-assessment ✔ = I did well ✗ = I need more practice
PET preparation diary		
I began preparing for PET on: (date)		
1 completed on		Reading Listening Speaking Writing Vocabulary Grammar
2 completed on		Reading Listening Speaking Writing Vocabulary Grammar
3 completed on		Reading Listening Speaking Vocabulary Grammar
4 completed on		Reading Listening Speaking Writing Vocabulary Grammar
5 completed on		Reading Listening Speaking Writing Vocabulary
6 completed on		Reading Listening Speaking Writing Vocabulary
7 completed on		Reading Listening Speaking Vocabulary Grammar
8 completed on		Reading Listening Speaking Vocabulary Grammar
9 completed on		Reading Speaking Writing Vocabulary Grammar
10 completed on		Reading Listening Speaking Writing Vocabulary Grammar
I am taking PET on: (test date)		

Personal information

1 | **Writing**

Complete this form with information about yourself.

> **PERSONAL FACTFILE**
>
> Name: ....
>
> Surname: ....
>
> Address: ....
>
> ....
>
> Sex: ....
>
> Age: ....
>
> Occupation: ....
>
> Interests: ....
>
> ....
>
> ....
>
> ....

2 | **Listening**

1 Listen to two people talking about themselves and complete their personal factfiles.

> **PERSONAL FACTFILE**
>
> Name: ....
>
> Surname: ....
>
> Address: ....
>
> ....
>
> Sex: ....
>
> Age: ....
>
> Occupation: ....
>
> Interests: ....
>
> ....
>
> ....
>
> ....

A

> **PERSONAL FACTFILE**
>
> Name: ....
>
> Surname: ....
>
> Address: ....
>
> ....
>
> Sex: ....
>
> Age: ....
>
> Occupation: ....
>
> Interests: ....
>
> ....
>
> ....

B

2 If you wanted to find out more information about these people, what questions would you ask? Make questions beginning with each of these words.

Are... ?

What... ?

When... ?

Do... ?

How... ?

Where... ?

3 Speaking

1 Look at the activities in the box. Which of these activities are you good at? Order the activities from most interesting (1) to least interesting (12).

Talk about why you like (1) and why you dislike (12).

watching sports	playing sports	computer games
watersports	collecting things	playing a musical instrument
dancing	learning languages	making things
driving	keep-fit exercises	surfing the Internet

2 David and Victoria have just met at a party. Complete the gaps in their conversation using the phrases below. Write the correct letters in the spaces.

David: Hello. I'm David.
Victoria: **(1)** ....
David: Yes, I'm one of his friends too, and we play football together. What do you study?
Victoria: **(2)** ....
David: I've finished college, actually, and I'm working as a windsurfing instructor.
Victoria: **(3)** ....
David: That doesn't matter. You could learn.
Victoria: **(4)** ....
David: So am I. I'm running a course which starts next week. Would you be interested in joining?
Victoria: **(5)** ....

Use five of these phrases to complete Victoria's part of the conversation.

A English. Have you finished college?
B Yes, I suppose so. But what I'm really interested in is sailing.
C Hi. I'm Victoria. I'm a friend of Tom's from college.
D Hello, I'm Victoria. I'm really interested in football.
E I'm doing languages. What about you? ·
F Oh, I'm really interested in watersports, but I'm not very good at windsurfing.
G Oh... I might be... it depends.

3 Which two didn't you use? Now listen and check.

4 When you meet someone of your own age for the first time:

• what questions do you ask them?
• what are good things to talk about?
• what do you tell them about yourself?

4 Writing

You have decided to join an English-language club on the Internet. Write a brief description of yourself for the database. You can write up to 100 words. Remember to include:

• your personal details, for example, name and age
• what you do/study
• the things that you are interested in

5 **Listening** Listen to these people giving personal information. As you listen, make a note of their names, addresses and telephone numbers.

Person	Name	Address	Telephone number
1			
2			
3			
4			
5			

6 **Grammar** **Finish the second sentence so that it means the same as the first.**

1 Do you play football well?
   Are you..

2 Do watersports interest you?
   Are you..

3 What is your age?
   How ....

4 Where exactly do you live?
   What is...

5 How is your surname spelt?
   How do you ....

7 **Reading** 1 **Look at these notices and choose the correct explanation, A, B, C, or D.**

Notice 1 is telling you: **1**
A where to write.
B what to write about.
C which type of letters to use.
D which type of pen to use.

> Please write in
> BLOCK CAPITALS

Notice 2 is giving you: **2**
A some advice.
B a suggestion.
C an instruction.
D a warning.

> **ALL PACKAGES**
> **MUST BE**
> **SIGNED FOR**

2 **What is a signature? How is it different from other ways of writing your name?**
Write your name in block capitals: ....
Write your signature: ....

1 Vocabulary

1 Match the words in A with the words in B. For example, *comb* and *hair* go together. Some words are used more than once.

A

attend	boil	brush	clean	comb
dial	dust	feed	iron	miss
tidy	tie	wash		

B

bus	class	desk	dishes
furniture	hair	meeting	number
pet	shirt	shoes	
shoelaces	teeth	water	

Which of these things do you do regularly, sometimes, occasionally, or never? Talk about some of your habits using the words in the boxes.

2 Now match the words in C with the words in D. Some words are used more than once.

C

hand in	join in	take off
put on	put up	put away
turn up	plug in	turn on

D

books	game	homework
make-up	music	radio
socks	umbrella	light

Use the words in the boxes to talk about your daily life.

2 Writing

Do you like listening to the radio? Why? Why not?
- An international radio station wants to find out about its listeners.
- You have agreed to complete a questionnaire for the radio station.
- Look at the questionnaire and answer each question.

Radio Good Times
22 Coast Road,
Brighton BN21 5AH, UK

Please tell us about yourself:

Full name: **(1)** ....

Home address: **(2)** ....

Nationality: **(3)** ....

Date of birth (day/month/year): **(4)**...

Occupation: **(5)**..

How many hours a week do you listen to the radio? **(6)** ....

What type of radio programme do you listen to most? **(7)**....................................

Where do you listen to the radio? **(8)** ....

What activities do you do while listening? **(9)** ....

Which famous English-speaking person would you like us to interview

on the radio? **(10)**..

Thank you for answering our questions!

Get ready for PET Writing Part 2

1 You should complete the questionnaire giving real information about yourself. However, if you never listen to the radio, imagine that you do and invent answers to questions 6–10.

2 Write about one to four words (or figures) in each space.

3 For question 2, don't forget to include the name of your country.

4 For question 3, if, for example, you come from Spain, your nationality is Span*ish*.If you come from Brazil, your nationality is Brazil*ian*. Make sure you spell your nationality correctly and use a capital letter.

5 For question 5, write what you do. For example, *student*, *accountant*, or *unemployed*.

6 Look at the questionnaire below. None of the answers is satisfactory. Why not?

Radio Good Times
22 Coast Road,
Brighton BN21 5AH, UK

Please tell us about yourself:

Full name: **(1)** .... *Ralf* ....

Home address: **(2)** .... *Berlin* ....

Nationality: **(3)** .... *Germany* ....

Date of birth (day/month/year): **(4)**............................... *july 1987* ....

Occupation: **(5)**............................... *school* ....

How many hours a week do you listen to the radio? **(6)** .... *200* ....

What type of radio programme do you listen to most? **(7)**............... *TV* ....

Where do you listen to the radio? **(8)** .... *no* ....

What activities do you do while listening? **(9)** .... *car* ....

Which famous English-speaking person would you like us to interview on the radio? **(10)**............................... *Napoleon Bonaparte* ....

Thank you for answering our questions!

---

3 Grammar

There are several ways to make comparisons.
Examples:
*Sam listens to the radio **more** often **than** Marcia does.*
*Marcia listens to the radio **less** often **than** Sam does.*
*Marcia doesn't listen to the radio **as** often **as** Sam does.*

*My shoes are clean**er than** my brother's.*
*My brother's shoes are dirt**ier than** mine.*
*My brother's shoes aren't **as** clean **as** mine.*

*My grandmother is **better** at ironing **than** my mother.*
*My mother is not **as** good at ironing **as** my grandmother.*
*My mother is **worse** at ironing **than** my grandmother.*

Finish the second sentence so that it means the same as the first.

1 Your bedroom is tidier than mine.
My bedroom isn't ....

2 Gerry doesn't do the washing-up as fast as Paul.
Paul does the washing-up ....

3 The new armchair isn't nearly as comfortable as the old one.
The old armchair is much ....

4 Every evening, Sally does a lot more homework than Rachel.
Every evening, Rachel does a lot ....

5 This music isn't nearly as bad as the music they play on Radio 2.
The music they play on Radio 2 is far ....

4 Reading

1 **What inventions of the last 2,000 years have caused the most important changes in people's daily lives?**

2 **Read this text and choose the correct word, A, B, C or D for each space.**

INVENTIONS OF THE LAST 2,000 YEARS

Recently, hundreds of scientists and philosophers were asked to name the most important invention of the last 2,000 years. You might **(1)** .... people to say the Internet, penicillin or the internal combustion engine, but in **(2)** .... nobody did. One scientist **(3)** .... for paper because, long before the Internet, paper allowed ideas to be sent around the world. **(4)** .... scientists agreed that modern medicine has helped millions of people, but said **(5)** .... inventions, such as soap and pipes for clean and dirty water, have **(6)** .... more lives. One philosopher said hay was the most important because it's winter food for horses. Without **(7)** .... , horses couldn't exist in cold climates, **(8)** .... meant that there couldn't be cities in places colder than Athens and Rome. So, thanks **(9)** .... hay, Vienna, Paris, London and Berlin were built! Someone else named the mirror because in **(10)** .... at our own faces we can learn about human beings in general.

1	**A** expect	**B** think	**C** believe	**D** guess
2	**A** all	**B** fact	**C** particular	**D** detail
3	**A** suggested	**B** judged	**C** answered	**D** voted
4	**A** Other	**B** Another	**C** Others	**D** Any
5	**A** clearer	**B** plainer	**C** simpler	**D** purer
6	**A** rescued	**B** delivered	**C** saved	**D** recovered
7	**A** them	**B** it	**C** these	**D** many
8	**A** what	**B** that	**C** where	**D** which
9	**A** to	**B** of	**C** by	**D** from
10	**A** seeing	**B** looking	**C** watching	**D** studying

You live and learn

1 Vocabulary

1 Look at the photographs.

A

B

In which of the photos can you see these things?

mouse	screen	desk
blackboard	keyboard	pen
chair	map	

somebody...
  asking   thinking
  talking   reading
  explaining   waiting

2 What other things can you see in the photographs?

2 Speaking

1 Look at these ideas. Which five do you think are the best ways to learn English?

surfing the Internet   listening to songs
studying a textbook   **?**   watching satellite TV
      going to classes   talking to people in English
    playing computer games   watching films in English
          doing grammar exercises   reading newspapers and magazines

2 Listen to Polly. She is studying Spanish.
- Which is her favourite way of studying Spanish?
- Choose the correct picture.

A ☐   B ☐   C ☐   D ☐

- Why does Polly like studying in this way?

3 You want to ask Polly about the things in the box below. Write the questions.

the teacher	length of each class	number of students
the book(s) and equipment	type of people	cost of course
the classroom	number of classes per week	what she's learnt

Get ready for PET Speaking Part 1

1 In the exam you have to *talk to your partner*.
2 Before the exam, you need lots of practice in *asking* questions correctly.
3 When you *answer* questions, say what you think and explain why.
4 Make the conversation *interesting*, add extra information, ask questions, and react to what your partner says.

3 Speaking

1 Look at this situation.
A young friend of yours wants to learn a new language in his free time.
He has a small amount of money to spend on this new hobby.
First, talk about the things he can buy to help him learn the language.
Then, say which will be the best use of his money.

Get ready for PET Speaking Part 2

1 Listen to the instructions. Are you talking about yourself or somebody else?
2 Speak to your partner, not to the examiner.
3 Remember to *listen* to your partner and *respond* to what (s)he says.
4 Say *what* you think and explain *why* you think it.

Examples:
I think x is a good idea because...
I think x is better than y because...
I think (s)he should buy x because...
I think the best thing (for him/her) to buy is x because...

2 Pietro and Valerie are doing exercise 3.1. Complete the gaps in their conversation using the phrases below. Write the correct letters in the spaces.

Valerie: So, our friend wants to learn a new language?

Pietro: **(1)** ....

Valerie: No, he can't. Let's start by talking about which of them will be useful for him.

Pietro: **(2)** ....

Valerie: OK. Shall we start with this one, the dictionary?

Pietro: **(3)** ....

Valerie: Yes, I agree, and it's also good for checking spelling. But what about a textbook? They're useful too.

Pietro: **(4)** ....

Valerie: Possibly. Or he may get one free when he pays for the course.

Pietro: **(5)** ....

Use five of these phrases to complete Pietro's part of the conversation.

A Oh yes, that's a good point.

B I don't like them very much.

C Yes they are, but maybe he won't need one because he'll have a teacher.

D Would you like a dictionary or a textbook?

E OK, then afterwards we can decide which one he should buy.

F That's right, and he's only got £20 to spend, so he can't buy all these things, can he?

G Yes, I think he should buy one of those, because it's very useful if you don't know what words mean.

3 Which two phrases didn't you use? Now listen and check.

4 Listening

- Look at these five statements.
- Listen to Tim and Janet talking about the courses they are doing in their free time.
- Decide if each statement is correct or incorrect.
- If you think it is correct, put a tick (✓) in the box under **A** for **Yes**. If you think it is not correct, put a tick (✓) in the box under **B** for **No**.

	A	B
	Yes	**No**
1 Janet thinks her computer classes are too long.	☐	☐
2 Tim has learnt many new things on his course.	☐	☐
3 Tim has to buy the food he cooks on his course.	☐	☐
4 Tim asks Janet to help him with his cookery.	☐	☐
5 Janet agrees to help Tim solve a problem.	☐	☐

5 Grammar

Finish the second sentence so that it means the same as the first.

1 Each lesson is two hours long.

Each lesson lasts ....

2 What's the price of this CD ROM, please?

How ....

3 I think a dictionary is very useful.

In my ....

4 I think that you are right about the textbook.

I agree ....

5 What about talking about the videotape first?

Let's ....

All the best books

1 Reading

Read the notices and answer the questions.
- Which one can you probably see in **a)** a library? **b)** a bookshop?
- Which one is **a)** advertising something? **b)** warning you?
- What does each notice mean? Choose **A**, **B**, **C** or **D**.

1

> Just published -
>
> **Mediterranean Cookery**
> by **Poppy Tobin**
>
> *Signed copies available on request*

A We have published all of Poppy Tobin's books about cooking.

B Watch someone give a cooking demonstration here today.

C Sign here if you'd like a copy of Poppy Tobin's latest book.

D Buy a new book with the writer's signature in it here.

2

> Please respect all books in your care.
>
> Heavy fines for any damage to borrowed books.

A Take care when looking at damaged books.

B You'll have to pay if you don't look after our books.

C It's fine to borrow these books except for the heavy ones.

D You can use these books here, but you can't borrow them.

2 Vocabulary

Look at these book covers. What type of book do you think each one is? Choose your answers from the words in the box.

mystery	romance	horror	science fiction
thriller	biography	humour	travel

Which of these books would you like to read? Why do you enjoy this type of book?

A   B   C   D

E   F   G   H

3 Reading

The people in 1–5 all want to buy a book.
- Look at the descriptions of eight books (A–H).
- Decide which one would be most suitable for each person.

1 Laura is looking for a book for her grandson's fifth birthday present. Preferably, it should be about space travel or animals and be a story she can read to him many times.

2 Moira's 14-year-old daughter loves science fiction videos. Moira wants to encourage her to read more by giving her a book which will hold her attention.

3 Fiona, like everyone in her family, is very interested in the cinema and enjoys reading about it. She wants a book that will give her all the gossip about film stars past and present.

4 James, who is 15, is looking for something to pass the time on a long plane journey. He'd like to read an adventure story which brings a period of history to life.

5 Gerry likes mystery stories which are full of suspense and excitement. He'd prefer to buy a book by a new writer.

This week's bargain books

A   The Meeting
This exciting novel is aimed at teenagers but adults will enjoy it, too. It's the 16th century and Per, the farm boy, rescues a princess. There are marvellous chases, battle scenes and romantic meetings – you couldn't ask for more thrilling action in a story, or a more realistic picture of the past.

B   Stealing Scenes
Starting at the age of five, the writer of this amusing autobiography has had a long and successful career as an actress on stage and screen. She takes us into her world of lights and cameras and tells the secrets of famous people she has known.

C   The Bucketful of Dinosaurs
When Harry finds a bucketful of dinosaurs, he's delighted and takes them everywhere he goes until one day he leaves them on a train. How will he prove that the dinosaurs belong to him? Very young children will never get tired of listening to this charming adventure.

D   Blood Rain
In this seventh book in the series about an Italian police inspector, the hero investigates a murder. The victim? Maybe just a friendless nobody, or perhaps the son of the country's most powerful criminal. Can the inspector manage both to find the murderer and to stay alive?

E   Hex Shadows
This story is set in the year 2367 when Britain is a part of the cruel European Federation. Hexes, human computers who were created in the late 21st century, are now hunted down as enemies of the Federation. This is an exciting, fast-moving story which teenagers will love.

F   Space Age
Designed with the fact-hungry child in mind, this gives information about stars, galaxies, astronauts and spaceships. It will bring the universe to life and make science and technology fun for those between five and ten years old.

G   Stormy Weather
This thriller is the first from the pen of a young Canadian. It follows the story of Dale, a meteorologist who is invited on a small plane to watch a thunderstorm. Dale soon discovers that not all dangers come from nature, and to save his life he must find the answers to some deadly questions.

H   Shoot!
For more than 20 years, this has been recognized as the best guide to the movies. This latest edition gives details and opinions about more than 22,000 films. It tells you about video availability, which films are suitable for family viewing, and the prizes films have won.

Get ready for PET Reading Part 2

1 Look at the information about Laura. Underline the words that are important about her.
Have you underlined: *grandson's fifth birthday*, *space travel or animals* and *read... many times*?

2 Which book would be suitable for a child of five (*grandson's fifth birthday*)? Are A, B or E suitable? Why not?
What about C and F? Why? (*very young children, those between five and ten years old*)

3 Are C and F about *space travel* or *animals*? Remember, dinosaurs are animals.

4 C and F can't both be suitable. Which one is unsuitable? Why? So which is the most suitable book for Laura?

5 Now do the same for the other people.

4 Vocabulary

Harry had a *bucketful* of dinosaurs. Complete these sentences in an interesting way.

1 Brian can't speak because he's just taken a mouthful of ....

2 You won't get better unless you swallow this spoonful of ....

3 When nobody was looking, Katia gave me a handful of ....

4 Graham felt hungry when he looked at the plateful of ....

5 Jenny's jacket was heavy because she had a pocketful of ....

5 Writing

Write this letter:

• You have an English friend called Lucy.

• Last week, Lucy lent you her favourite book, but while you had the book it was damaged.

• Now you want to write a short letter to Lucy about the damaged book.

• In your letter, apologize for the damage, explain how it happened, and offer to do something about it. Write about 100 words.

Dear Lucy,
Something terrible has happened. ....
....

Here are some useful phrases that you can use in your writing.

To apologize to someone, you can write:

I'm very sorry I didn't look after your book very well.
Please forgive me.

To explain the order in which something happened, you can write:

First (this happened), next (that happened), then (something else happened), and finally (this happened).

To offer to do something for someone, you can write:

I'll buy you a new one.
I can mend it for you.
If you like, I'll give you mine.
Let me help you.

Holiday adventures

1 Reading

Read these notices. Which one can you see a) in a travel agency window? b) at an airport? c) in a hotel?

1

Find out about excursions, nightlife and transport to the airport at our 24-hour reception desk

2

70,000 package holidays
Reservations 9 am - 6 pm

Leave an answerphone message outside these hours

3

Do not leave your luggage unattended at any time

What does each notice mean? Choose A, B, C or D.

A Make sure there's always someone with your belongings.
B Ask the receptionist if you want your suitcases carried downstairs.
C You can make a booking here during the day.
D Someone is always available to give you information.

2 Speaking

1 Look at picture A and answer these questions. Use the words in the box.
1 Who can you see in the picture?
2 Where is she?
3 What's she doing?
4 What things can you see in the picture?
5 How does the girl probably feel? Why?

suitcase	young	wearing	packing
bedroom	nervous	clothes	holiday
quilt	abroad	plastic	woman

A

2 Now use your answers to describe the picture.
Begin: *This picture shows a young woman in her bedroom. She's ...*

3 Now look at picture B. Describe what you can see in the picture. Talk about:
* where the picture was taken
* the people
* what they are doing
* the things you can see
* what they are probably talking about

Use these words:

jacket	phone	writing
curly	arrangements	brochures
discussing	travel agency	shelf
desk	trip	pen

B

Begin: *This picture shows two people in a travel agency. They're ...*

3 Reading

1 How many of these questions do you answer with 'Yes'?

- Are you interested in wildlife and beautiful scenery?
- Do you enjoy camping?
- Do you prefer to go on holiday with a large group of people?
- Would you like to travel in foreign countries?

If you've answered 'Yes' four times, then you'd probably like the kind of holiday shown below. Do you agree? Why or why not?

2 Read the text to decide if each statement is correct or incorrect.

1 In a safari truck, passengers take it in turns to sit next to a window.
2 Safari trucks are able to travel over all types of roads.
3 Safari team leaders have a minimum of 12 months' touring experience.
4 The second driver is as experienced as the team leader.
5 Each truck comes supplied with all the food needed for the trip.
6 Everyone is expected to help get meals ready.
7 What people pay for their food depends on how much they eat.
8 There is always enough clean drinking water.
9 Campers have plenty of space in their tents.
10 Hot showers are provided for campers wherever they stop for the night.

Safari Holidays

If you want to get really close to the wildlife and scenery of Africa, then a Safari Holiday offers the most excitement and best value for money.

The Right Trucks for Africa

Each of our safari trucks is a safe, reliable vehicle which is suited to African travel conditions and allows you to fully enjoy the areas visited. Every seat is a window seat and the sides of the truck can be rolled up to provide a wide space for looking out. We use four-wheel-drive vehicles because roads can be rough or get washed away, and we don't want to be prevented from visiting interesting areas.

The Safari Team

Three of our employees go on each safari trip, one of whom is the team leader. All safari team leaders are fully trained and have worked for at least a year on a wide variety of trips in Africa before they lead their first safari. The team leader is a driver, mechanic, guide, diplomat and general expert on Africa. He is helped by a second driver, usually a team leader in training. The third member of the team, the cook, is as important as the leader. He or she sees that all cooking and camp tasks are completed as smoothly as possible.

Good Food

Safari Holidays are famous for their open-fire cooking. We stop regularly to buy fresh fruit, vegetables and meat in local markets and we also have a good supply of things like tea, coffee, dried milk and tinned food in the truck. All the members of the tour lend a hand with the food preparation and washing-up, under the experienced eye of the team cook. At the beginning of each trip, everyone, including the safari team members, pays the same amount of money into the safari purse and this covers food expenses. All water carried on the truck is safe to drink and we make sure it never runs out.

Quality Camping Equipment

Each truck carries everything needed for the trip. This includes four-person tents, used for only two people, air beds, mosquito nets, camp chairs, a fire grill for campfire cooking and all necessary cooking equipment, a cool box for storing fresh food, binoculars, books on Africa and a first-aid kit.

Accommodation

On Safari Holidays, we sometimes camp in an official campsite and sometimes we put up our tents in wild areas. Some campsites have very basic or no facilities, while at others hot showers and cold drinks are available. At the start or finish of tours, we usually have a night in a hotel. These are clean, comfortable and reasonably priced.

1 Don't worry about the meaning of every word. You don't have to understand every word in the text, only the ones which help you do the task.
2 Use the headings to help you find the answers. In which paragraphs can you find the answers to statements 4, 6, and 9?
3 Underline the words in the text which help you with each statement. What words will you underline for statements 1, 3, and 8?

4 Decide if the words in the text and the statement have the same meaning. Look at number 1. Does *Passengers take it in turns to sit next to a window* mean the same as *Every seat is a window seat*? What about number 2? Does the statement mean the same as the sentence which begins *We use four-wheel-drive vehicles...*?

4 Grammar

There are several ways to say *when* something happens.
Examples:
*Safari drivers must work for a year **before** they can become team leaders.*
*Safari drivers can become team leaders **after** they have worked for a year.*
*Safari drivers can't become team leaders **until** they have worked for a year.*

***When** the campers have put up their tents, they start cooking dinner.*
*The campers start cooking dinner **as soon as** they have put up their tents.*

*Safari members make a lot of new friends **while** they're on holiday.*
*Safari members make a lot of new friends **during** their holiday.*

Finish the second sentence so that it means the same as the first.

1 Learn to ski before you go on a winter holiday in the mountains.
Don't go on a winter holiday in the mountains until ....

2 When we arrived at the hotel, we immediately went for a swim.
We went for a swim as ....

3 We went sightseeing after lunch.
We went sightseeing during ....

4 During my holiday in Paris, I spoke a lot of French.
I spoke a lot of French while I ....

5 Don't book your holiday until you've seen my photos of Africa.
You must see my photos of Africa before ....

5 Vocabulary

You can use the words in the box when you're talking about holidays. Divide them into the six groups.

hotel countryside
sunglasses shells
plane taking photos
swimming coach
postcards train
guest house car
sunbathing tent
suntan lotion
handicrafts beach
guidebook picnics

Transport	Accommodation	Scenery	Activities	Things to pack	Souvenirs
car	hotel	beach	swimming	sunglasses	postcards

Think of words which describe the kind of holiday you like most. Use a dictionary to help you. Add the words to the table.

6 Speaking

Talk about the kind of holidays you like and don't like.

Just the job

3 2

1 **Speaking**

Look at the people in the photo. They're all going to work.

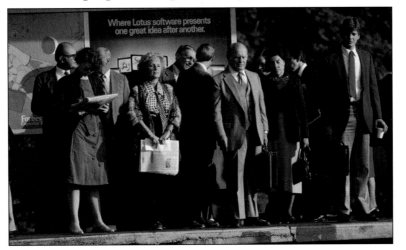

- What do you think each person does?
- Which person earns the highest salary?
- Which person gets on well with his or her colleagues?
- Which person is responsible for a large staff?
- Which person is planning to go on strike?

2 **Vocabulary**

1 Many people have to study for several years before they take up a profession or job. For example, an *architect* has studied *architecture*, and a *doctor* has studied *medicine*. What have these people studied?

Profession	Subject studied
architect	*architecture*
doctor	*medicine*
lawyer	
artist	
cook	
engineer	
tourist guide	
hairdresser	
journalist	
business man/woman	
actor/actress	
chemist	
biologist	
physicist	
musician	

2 Look at these verbs. You can make nouns by changing the end of each one. Complete the table.

Verb	Noun
apply	*application*
organize	
qualify	
decide	
operate	
employ	*employment*
advertise	
govern	
manage	
retire	
insure	
succeed	

Use the pairs of words to make sentences.
Example:
If you want to apply for a job, you have to fill in an application form.

3 Listening 👂 **1** You will hear four women talking about their jobs. Listen and complete the information in the table.

Speaker	Clothes	Equipment	Place	Activity
1				controlling traffic
2			advertising agency	
3		microscope		
4				

Listen again and match the speakers with the pictures, A, B, C or D.

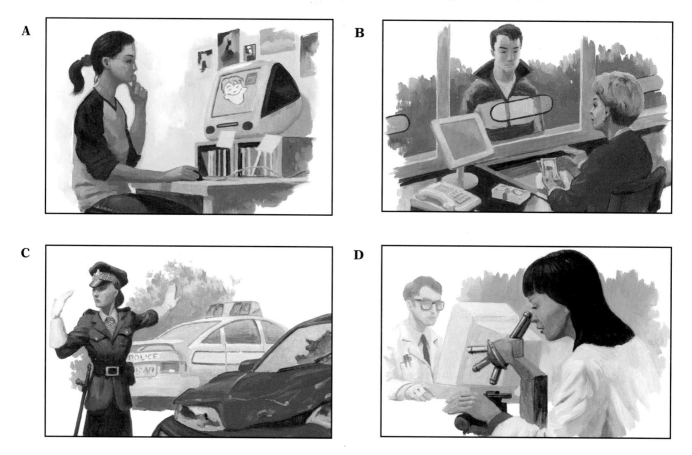

A

B

C

D

2 You will hear a woman talking on the radio about her job. Put a tick (✓) in the correct box for each question.

1 Where does Amanda usually work?
A ☐ in a restaurant
B ☐ in her own kitchen
C ☐ in other people's homes
D ☐ in recording studios

2 People are satisfied with Amanda's service because
A ☐ she provides large meals.
B ☐ she cooks healthy food.
C ☐ she gives people a wide choice.
D ☐ she prepares unusual dishes.

3 Amanda finds her job stressful if she
A ☐ has to cook for vegetarians.
B ☐ has to work in unsuitable places.
C ☐ doesn't know how many people to cook for.
D ☐ doesn't know when she should serve a meal.

4 What does Amanda enjoy most about her job?
A ☐ meeting famous bands
B ☐ being her own boss
C ☐ working for young people
D ☐ earning a lot of money

5 How does Amanda get to the place where she works?
A ☐ by car
B ☐ by bus
C ☐ by bike
D ☐ on foot

6 When she gets home in the evening, Amanda
A ☐ writes about cooking.
B ☐ cooks for her family.
C ☐ makes a shopping list.
D ☐ listens to music.

Get ready for PET Listening Part 2

1 Read the questions quickly before you hear the tape, so you know what to listen for.
2 You will hear the recording twice. If you miss the answer to a question, don't worry. Forget that question and think about the next one. You can find the answer when you hear the tape for a second time.
3 The answer to a question may not be in exactly the same words as the ones you hear. For example, what's the answer to question 2? What words does Amanda use to express this idea?.

4 For each question, A, B, C and D will seem possible, but only one will be right. For example, what is the answer to question 5? Amanda talks about the other kinds of transport but they are not how she gets to work. What does she say about each kind of transport?
5 Remember to check all your answers when you listen to the tape for a second time.

House and home

1 Which rooms do you have in your house?

dining room	kitchen	bedroom	garage
living room	bathroom	hallway	balcony
garden	stairs	storeroom	basement

Do you have any other rooms in your house?

2 In which room do you usually find these things? Divide them into the four groups. Some words can be used more than once.

dishwasher	wardrobe	chest of drawers	sink
coffee table	washbasin	armchair	dressing table
television	lamp	fridge	shower
cooker	towel rail	mirror	sofa

Living room	Kitchen	Bathroom	Bedroom

1 In the Speaking test, you talk about a photograph. If you don't know the English word for something, you can say what it:
- is used for
- is made of
- looks like

a) What's it used for? Read the example and complete 1–2.
Example:

What's a coffee table?
It's a small, low table which you usually find in the living room. You can put things like cups of coffee, newspapers and magazines on it.

1 What's a chest of drawers?
It's a small piece of furniture which ....
2 What's a towel rail?
It's..

b) What's it made of? Read the example and complete 1–2.
Example:

A wardrobe is usually made of wood.

1 A towel is usually ....
2 A frying pan is...

c) What's the difference? Read the example and complete 1–2.
Example:

dishwasher/washing machine
They are both machines which you usually find in the kitchen. A dishwasher is for washing plates, cups, etc. and a washing machine is for washing clothes.

1 cushions/pillows
2 curtains/blinds

2 **Choose one of the photographs and describe the room.**

A

B

Use the words in the box to help you talk about:

- the type of room it is
- what you can see in the room
- where the things are
- your opinion of the room
- who you think lives there

there's a/some
on top of
next to/beside
underneath/below
to the right of
to the left of
behind
in front of

3 **Listening** **1** **Listen to a boy describing his room. Which room is his?**

A ☐ B ☐ C ☐ D ☐

2 **Listen to a girl describing her home. Where does she live?**

A ☐ B ☐ C ☐ D ☐

3 **Describe your house. Talk about:**

- where it is
- what it looks like
- how many rooms it has
- your favourite room

4 Listening

Get ready for PET Listening Part 1

Remember:
1 the pictures may be partly right and partly wrong.
2 only one picture is completely right.
3 you hear everything twice.

1 **Look at the four pictures. Where is the calculator in each picture? Listen and decide which picture, A, B, C, or D, matches what you hear.**

A ☐   B ☐   C ☐   D ☐

2 **What time does the man's bus leave?**

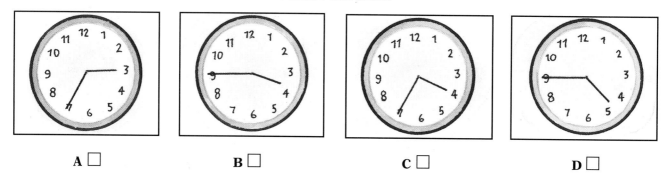

A ☐   B ☐   C ☐   D ☐

3 **What does the woman decide to eat?**

A ☐   B ☐   C ☐   D ☐

4 **Which piece of equipment does the woman need?**

A ☐   B ☐   C ☐   D ☐

Interesting people

1 Vocabulary

1 How often does your family get together for a celebration? Do you enjoy family parties? Why? Why not?

2 Find someone in the photo who:

is bald	has long hair	is in a white dress	is smiling
is middle-aged	looks bored	is wearing a hat	is dancing

Now describe the photo. Begin like this:

'This is a picture of a family party. There are a lot of people here. Most of them are sitting down at long tables, but some people...'

3 The words in the boxes describe people. In the first box, find seven pairs of words with *opposite* meanings.

attractive	careful	careless	cheerful	confident	miserable	foolish
hard-working	lazy	shy	strong	ugly	weak	wise

4 In this box, find seven pairs of words with *similar* meanings.

amusing	anxious	blond	boring	understanding	dull	fair
funny	honest	patient	slim	thin	truthful	worried

5 Which words describe you?

2 Writing

Write this letter.
- You recently went to a party and made two new friends.
- Now you are writing a letter to an English friend.
- Explain who you met at the party, describe what they looked like, and say why you liked them.
- Write about 100 words.

Complete these sentences and use them in your letter.

I noticed X and Y as soon as I went into the room because ....

It's the first time I've met people who ....

X isn't good-looking but ....

Y was wearing ....

X and I liked each other immediately because ....

I got on well with Y because ....

Begin your letter like this:

Dear Sam,
I want to tell you about two people I met at a party last Saturday. ....
....

3 **Reading**

1 **Generally, how old are people when they first a) learn to read? b) go to university? Read the article about a boy who has done these things at a younger age than most people, and then answer the questions.**

The most difficult thing for university student Shaun Rogers is opening his classroom door. Shaun can't do this without help because he's only six years old. He's the youngest person ever to study at Rochester University in New York. Shaun began reading at two, by the age of five was regularly corresponding with university professors and will shortly complete his first book. 'I love learning,' says Shaun. 'My hero is the scientist Albert Einstein because he never combed his hair or wore socks.'

Psychologists have found it difficult to test Shaun's intelligence because it goes beyond what they usually measure. Shaun's mother first realized her son was different when he kept crying at playschool because he was bored with the children's games. She started teaching him at home after finding that local schools were not prepared for children who learnt at Shaun's speed. Now Shaun is studying geography at Rochester University and using the Internet to complete his high school studies.

However, some psychologists warn that too much study can prevent a child from developing normally. 'I don't care how brilliant the kid is, six-year-olds have to play with their friends,' says Dr Brian Wood. Mrs Rogers disagrees that her son's time is completely taken up by school work. 'He loves the violin and has many outdoor interests, such as camping, fishing and swimming, just like other boys his age.'

1 What is the writer trying to do in the text?
A advise parents about their children's education
B compare the development of normal and clever children
C encourage students to enter university at a young age
D interest people in the life of an unusual child

2 What can a reader find out from this text?
A who Shaun's friends are
B when Shaun did an intelligence test
C what Shaun's hobbies are
D how well Shaun plays the violin

3 Why did Shaun's mother decide to educate him at home?
A because she couldn't find a suitable school for him
B because his school wouldn't let him use the Internet
C because his teachers were unkind and made him cry
D because he didn't get on with the other children

4 What does Dr Wood think about Shaun?
A He isn't really any cleverer than other six-year-olds.
B He should spend more time having fun with other children.
C He will have to study harder to succeed at university.
D He can help his friends to do better at school.

5 Which of these is Mrs Rogers talking about Shaun?

A 'My son gets bored easily if he doesn't have other children to play games or go swimming with him.'

B 'My son loves his studies and fortunately there are many children of his own age in his class who share his interests.'

C 'What makes my son different from other children is that he started studying earlier and learns things much more quickly.'

D 'Like most young boys, my son often looks untidy and spends more time using the Internet than doing his homework.'

Get ready for PET Reading Part 4

1 The first question on this kind of reading text asks you about the writer's purpose in writing the text.
Has the writer of the text about Shaun succeeded in her/his purpose? In other words, has s/he interested you in Shaun's life?

2 In this kind of reading text, you have to understand people's *attitudes* and *opinions* as well as factual information. From this text, what do you understand about:

- Shaun's *attitude* to studying?
- Dr Wood's *opinion* about what six-year-old children need to do?
- Mrs Rogers' *opinion* about the amount of time her son spends studying?

3 In some of the questions in this kind of reading text, you have to look for the answer in more than one place. Look at question 5 and underline the two places in the text which give you the correct answer.

2 Match the writer's purposes with the sentences.

1 to recommend something

2 to compare two things

3 to complain about something

4 to explain something

5 to warn against something

A Couples who decide to adopt a child should be prepared for the time when the child starts to ask difficult questions about the birth parents.

B Why do people using mobile phones in public places imagine everyone is interested in their conversations and speak in very loud voices?

C If, like me, you enjoy a film which keeps you sitting on the edge of your seat, then you shouldn't miss this one.

D I felt close to my grandmother because she always met me from school and listened while I described the events of my day.

E Children with several brothers and sisters may feel differently from an only child when it comes to the school holidays.

---

4 Grammar

Finish the second sentence so that it means the same as the first.

1 That teacher is very patient with her students.
That is the teacher ....

2 Shaun is too weak to open the classroom door.
Shaun isn't...

3 In our class, only a few students have curly hair.
In our class, not ....

4 My brother prefers funny films to serious ones.
My brother likes funny films ....

5 My grandmother's favourite film star is Tom Cruise.
Tom Cruise is the film star my grandmother ....

Places of interest

1 Reading

1 Look at the notices, 1–10. Would you find them in a museum, a sportscentre, a hotel, a giftshop or a post office?

1

Last collection:
19.30 Mon–Fri.

2

Changing rooms
this way

3

Rooms should be
vacated by 12.00

4

Ask for our
free gift-
wrapping
service

5

Parcels and heavy items
should be taken to window
7 for weighing

6

Please do not
touch the
exhibits

7

EQUIPMENT
CAN BE HIRED
BY THE HOUR

8

All breakages
must be paid for

9

Photocopying facilities
are available to guests
at Reception

10

A map of the display
areas is available at
the entrance

2 Look at each notice again. Is it:

a) giving you information about what facilities are available?
b) telling you what you must or mustn't do?
c) giving you simple information, for example where or when?

3 Choose one place from the box below. What type of notices would you expect to see there? Write two examples of each type, a), b) and c).

| school | department store | bank | airport |

2 Listening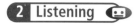

Get ready for PET Listening Part 3

1 In Part 3 of the PET Listening test, you have to listen and write the missing words in the gaps on the question paper.
2 The information on the page may be presented in different ways. Make sure you know what to do. Read the information on the page carefully and think about the type of information that is missing.

3 You don't have to understand every word – just listen for the missing information.
4 You will hear the words you need to write on the tape and you don't need to change them in any way. Don't worry if you're not sure how to spell the words correctly, but make sure you write clearly.
5 Don't write too much. One or two words is usually enough.

1 **Look at the notes about Orford Castle. Some information is missing.**

• You will hear a recorded message about the castle.
• For each question, fill in the missing information in the numbered space.

ORFORD CASTLE

Opening time:	(1) ....
Closing time:	4 pm
Price for adults:	£2.30
Price for children:	(2) ....
Telephone number:	(3) 01394 ....

In this example, the words on the left tell you what information you are listening for. Some of the information has already been completed. You only have to fill in the missing information where there is a number in brackets and a dotted line.

2 **Look at the notes about Framlingham Castle. Some information is missing.**

• You will hear a recorded message about the castle.
• For each question, fill in the missing information in the numbered space.

FRAMLINGHAM CASTLE

When you can go there:
Open between April and (1) ....
Open every day from 10.00 am to
(2) ....
What you can do there:
Walk around the (3) ....
Visit the (4) ....

In this example, the information is organized under headings. Again, some of the information is given and you just fill in the missing words.

3 **Look at the notes about Castle Rising. Some information is missing.**

• You will hear a recorded message about the castle.
• For each question, fill in the missing information in the numbered space.

CASTLE RISING

You can visit the castle any day between
(1) .... and Sunday.
There is a free (2) .... to give you
information about the castle.
In the giftshop, you can buy a
(3) .... as a souvenir of your visit.

In this example, the information about the castle is presented in the form of sentences. So, once again, some of the information is given and you just fill in the missing words.

3 Reading

Look at the statements about the trip to Arundel Castle. Read the text and decide if each statement is correct or incorrect.

1 Arundel Castle is in the same town as the Albion Hotel.
2 If you go on the trip, you may miss your evening meal at the hotel.
3 There is no charge for the journey to Arundel.
4 Arundel Castle is next to the river, in the centre of the town.
5 All of the castle buildings are less than 1,000 years old.
6 Part of the castle is in a poor condition.
7 Part of the castle is used as a private house.
8 It is necessary to book a table if you want to have lunch at the castle.
9 Afternoon tea at the castle is not very expensive.
10 To go on the trip, you have to reserve a place one day in advance.

BRITANNIA HOLIDAYS

Extra trip to Arundel Castle: Wednesday

Dear Holiday-maker,

I hope that you are enjoying your visit to the Albion Hotel. I'm writing to tell you about an extra trip we are arranging for Wednesday afternoon. We'll be going to Arundel Castle, which is a tourist attraction about 40 miles from here. A coach will be leaving at 11 am and returning in time for your evening meal at 7 pm. The kitchen has been informed so if we're late for any reason, they'll wait for us. Please remember this is not part of your package so, although the coach is free, there is an entrance fee of £7.00 if you want to visit the castle.

The town of Arundel is very pretty, with pleasant walks down by the river and some interesting old shops. The castle stands on a hill outside the town and can be seen from miles around. There has been a castle on this site for almost 1,000 years, but the present building is not that old, so it's certainly not an old ruin. The castle buildings are used as a home by the present owners, but quite a large part is open to the public.

Among the things to see at the castle are some lovely rooms. The library has a wonderful ceiling and there is a beautiful bedroom, once used by members of the royal family. There is furniture dating from the 16th century and a fine collection of old clocks, which shouldn't be missed. The picture gallery is also very interesting and has paintings by famous artists such as Canaletto and Gainsborough.

We will arrive in Arundel at lunchtime and the castle has its own restaurant, which serves excellent home-made lunches. If a group of you would like to pre-book, we can arrange a discount for you. If not, you can decide when you arrive and there are always plenty of free tables. For those of you who prefer a lighter meal, traditional English afternoon tea is served in the restaurant from 3.00 pm at a very reasonable price.

So, if you would like to join us on our trip to Arundel, please ask at Reception by Tuesday lunchtime at the latest, and your name will be added to the list.
Have a nice day.

Clara Tongue
Tour Company Representative

4 Speaking

1 **What are the main tourist attractions in your area**
• for young people?
• for older people?
• for foreign visitors?

2 **Talk about a historic building in your country and say what visitors can see and do there.**

Getting there

1 Vocabulary

1 Look at the words in the box. Divide them into four groups. Some of the words can be used more than once.

driver	pilot	attendant	land	catch	miss
get on	take off	check in	ticket	fare	station
take	platform	boarding pass	meter	timetable	gate

Taxi	Train	Bus/Coach	Plane

2 Complete the gaps in these sentences with words from the table.

1 If we don't hurry up, we'll .... the bus. It leaves the bus .... at ten o'clock.
2 It's cheaper for four people to .... a taxi rather than go on the underground, because the taxi .... comes to less than the price of four ....
3 After you .... your luggage, they give you a .... which you take along to the .... , where someone checks it before you .... the plane.
4 The train to Edinburgh leaves from .... number eight and you have to buy your .... in the office before you ....
5 In the .... , it said that the bus left at 10.00, and so we got there at 09.45 so that we would be sure to .... it.

2 Speaking

Look at the photograph and describe it. Make sure you answer these questions:
• Where was it taken? Who are the people? What is each of them doing? Why?
• What things can you see in the photograph?
• What are the people going to do next? Why?

What are the good and bad things about travelling by plane?

3 Reading

1 Look at these notices. On which type of transport would you expect to see each one?

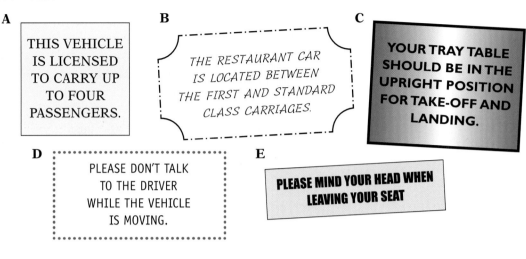

A

THIS VEHICLE
IS LICENSED
TO CARRY UP
TO FOUR
PASSENGERS.

B

THE RESTAURANT CAR
IS LOCATED BETWEEN
THE FIRST AND STANDARD
CLASS CARRIAGES.

C

YOUR TRAY TABLE
SHOULD BE IN THE
UPRIGHT POSITION
FOR TAKE-OFF AND
LANDING.

D

PLEASE DON'T TALK
TO THE DRIVER
WHILE THE VEHICLE
IS MOVING.

E

PLEASE MIND YOUR HEAD WHEN
LEAVING YOUR SEAT

Get ready for PET Reading Part 1

1 In Part 1 of the PET Reading test, there are five multiple-choice (**A**, **B**, **C**, or **D**) questions.
2 Remember that notices may be:
- telling you what to do or what not to do.
- telling you what is available.
- giving you information about things.

3 This is how to choose the correct explanation.
- First, look at the sign and imagine how you would explain it to a friend.
- Then look at the four explanations and choose the one which is closest to what you would say.
- Finally, check the other explanations and find words or phrases in the notice that tell you that these explanations are not correct.

2 Look at this notice. Choose the correct explanation, A, B, C or D.

Available 1st July.
One-bedroom furnished flat.
Reasonable rent.
Convenient for shops
and buses.

A I'm looking for somewhere to live.
B I'm looking for furniture for a flat.
C I'm looking for someone to live in a flat.
D I'm looking for someone who wants to buy a flat.

The answer to this question is C.
Which words tell you that this is the answer?
Which words tell you that **A** is not the answer?
Which words tell you that **B** is not the answer?
Which words tell you that **D** is not the answer?

3 Look at these notices and decide which is the correct explanation, A, B, C or D. Think about why your answer is correct and why the other explanations are not correct.

1

PLEASE SPEAK
QUIETLY IN THE
LIBRARY AREA.
PEOPLE ARE
STUDYING NEARBY.

A You are not allowed to talk here.
B You can only stay here if you are studying.
C You should try not to disturb people.
D You may only speak in certain parts of the library.

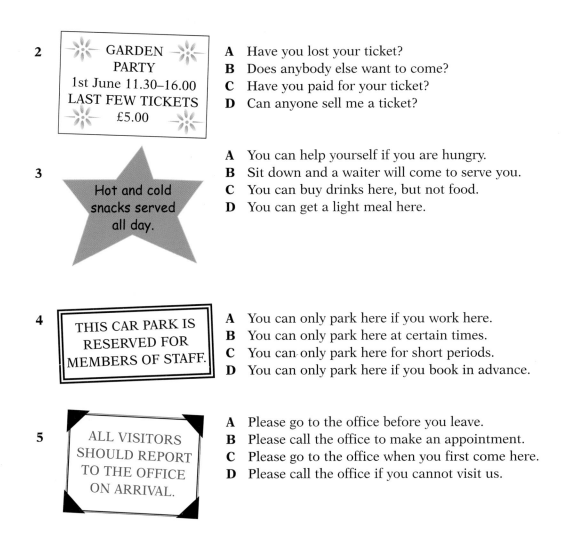

2 GARDEN PARTY
1st June 11.30–16.00
LAST FEW TICKETS
£5.00

A Have you lost your ticket?
B Does anybody else want to come?
C Have you paid for your ticket?
D Can anyone sell me a ticket?

3 Hot and cold snacks served all day.

A You can help yourself if you are hungry.
B Sit down and a waiter will come to serve you.
C You can buy drinks here, but not food.
D You can get a light meal here.

4 THIS CAR PARK IS RESERVED FOR MEMBERS OF STAFF.

A You can only park here if you work here.
B You can only park here at certain times.
C You can only park here for short periods.
D You can only park here if you book in advance.

5 ALL VISITORS SHOULD REPORT TO THE OFFICE ON ARRIVAL.

A Please go to the office before you leave.
B Please call the office to make an appointment.
C Please go to the office when you first come here.
D Please call the office if you cannot visit us.

4 Writing

You have been asked to complete a questionnaire about travelling in your country. Look at the questionnaire and answer each question.

TRAVEL QUESTIONNAIRE

1 Surname: ....

2 Forenames: ....

3 Home address: ....

4 Are you are a car driver? ....

5 How do you usually travel to work/school/college?...............

6 How many hours a week do you spend travelling? ....

7 What is good about the way you travel?............................

8 What is not so good about the way you travel?...................

9 What alternatives are available to you? ....

10 Signature: ....

Thank you for taking time to fill in this questionnaire.

What a bargain!

1 Vocabulary

What's the difference between these pairs of words?
Example:
A jacket is shorter than a coat.
Check your answers in a dictionary.

coat/jacket	shirt/skirt
boot/shoe	socks/tights
tie/belt	wool/cotton
collar/sleeve	spots/stripes
pocket/bag	zip/buttons

2 Reading

Read these notices. Match them with the correct explanation, A, B, C, or D.
There is one extra explanation.

1

> Changing rooms
> next to lift.
> Customers may take in no
> more than
> 4 pieces of clothing.

2

> Sorry!
> Lift to women's fashions
> out of order –
> Use escalator in TV
> department

3

> Today only!
> Prices on all
> electrical goods
> greatly reduced

A Because the lift isn't working, you'll have to go upstairs another way.
B You may not change any women's clothes you buy in today's sale.
C If you buy a television today, it will be much cheaper than usual.
D There's a limit to the number of clothes you may try on at one time.

3 Vocabulary

Read the sentences about money and find the missing words in the word square.
They are written from top to bottom, left to right, right to left and diagonally.
1 I don't _ _ _ _ a lot of money in my job, but I _ _ _ _ some every week for my holiday.
2 If you don't have cash, you can write a _ _ _ _ _ _ or pay by _ _ _ _ _ _ card.
3 If you don't put that _ _ _ _ in your wallet, and the _ _ _ _ in your pocket, you'll lose them before you can spend them!

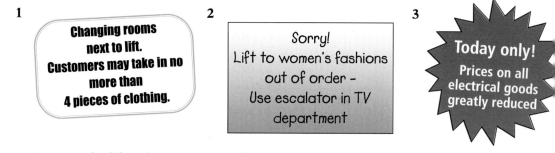

C	S	L	S	A	V	E
H	C	H	E	Q	U	E
A	O	R	O	N	X	A
R	I	W	E	P	D	R
G	N	X	E	D	I	N
E	T	O	N	P	I	T
R	E	C	E	I	P	T

4 I got a _ _ _ _ _ _ _ when I bought these books for you, so you can see how much money you _ _ _ me.
5 Some people will borrow money from you, but they'll never _ _ _ _ it to you!
6 People like to _ _ _ _ in big department stores because everything they want is under one roof.
7 How much do you _ _ _ _ _ _ to repair shoes?
8 The service was very good here, so I'm going to leave the waitress a large _ _ _ .

4 Writing

1 In PET Writing Part 3, you are asked to write a letter to an English-speaking friend. Look at this example writing task.

- On your birthday recently, you received a present from an English-speaking friend.
- Now you are writing a letter to this friend.
- Thank your friend for the present, invite your friend to visit a new shopping centre with you, and describe the shopping centre.
- Write about 100 words.

2 This is the letter one student wrote. Write the missing words.

Dear Chris,

Thank you very [1] .... for the birthday present [2] .... sent me. It [3] .... kind of you to remember [4] .... birthday. The sweater [5] .... me perfectly and I love the colour. I'm going [6] .... use the money my grandmother gave me to buy some new trousers to go [7] .... it.

Have you [8] .... to the new shopping centre yet? Why don't [9] .... go together this Saturday? I could come [10] .... your house at about 3 o'clock and then we could [11] .... the bus from the end [12] .... your street.

I know you'll like [13] .... shopping centre. It has a [14] .... of really good clothes shops, great music stores, and [15] .... enormous bookstore. There's a café [16] .... we can have ice cream, and, [17] .... we've got any money left, we [18] .... see a film at the cinema there.

I [19] .... you can come. Phone me or [20] .... me an e-mail.

Love,
Andrea

- How does Andrea thank Chris? What does Andrea say about the sweater?
- How does Andrea invite Chris?
- Look at these sentences. Find three invitations, one acceptance, and one refusal.
  Please come to the shopping centre with me.
  I'd really like you to come to the shopping centre with me.
  I'd love to go to the shopping centre with you.
  Would you like to come to the shopping centre with me?
  I'm afraid I can't go to the shopping centre with you.
- You make arrangements when you give an invitation. What arrangements does Andrea suggest?
- At the end of a letter, you write one or two 'goodbye' sentences.
  How does Andrea show the letter includes an invitation?
  What other 'goodbye' sentence does Andrea write?
- Look at these sentences. Find four 'goodbye' sentences and one 'hello' sentence.
  Please write soon.
  I'm sorry I haven't written for a long time.
  Thank you again for the lovely present.
  Give my love/best wishes to your family.
  See you soon.
- At the end of a letter, you always sign your name. What does Andrea write before the signature? Look at these phrases. Find two from an informal letter and one from a formal one.
  Yours sincerely,
  Best wishes,
  Yours,

1 Read the instructions carefully and imagine yourself in the situation.
2 In your letter, you are told to do three things. For example, in the letter to Chris, you have to *thank*, *invite* and *describe*. Make sure you follow the instructions for all three of them.
3 Your letter will look good if you write it in separate paragraphs, as Andrea has done. Start each paragraph on a new line.
4 Remember to write a 'goodbye' sentence and to sign your name.
5 Try not to write fewer than 100 words, but don't write many more than 100.
6 When you've written your letter, check it carefully. Make sure you've followed all the instructions. Correct any grammar and spelling mistakes.

3 **Write this letter.**

- You spent last Saturday with an English-speaking friend and this friend has just sent you some photos of the day.
- Now you are writing a letter to this friend.
- Thank your friend for the photos, invite your friend to visit a local tourist attraction with you next weekend, and describe what you can see and do there.
- Write about 100 words.

Dear Lesley,
I've just received the photos you took last Saturday. ....
....

5 **Listening** **Do you like shopping in street markets? Why? Why not?**
- Look at the advertisement for some street markets in London.
- Some information is missing.
- Listen to the man talking on the radio about the markets, and fill in the missing words.

East London Markets

Columbia Road
Over 50 stalls selling (1) .... at bargain prices.

Brick Lane
A market speciality is (2) ....

Petticoat Lane
Sells everything from clothes to toys. Busiest day is (3) ....

Whitechapel
It's opposite (4) .... Get your Asian vegetables and spices here.

Come and be part of the fun!

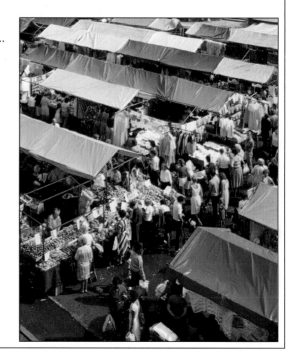

6 2 City life

1 Vocabulary

1 Look at these photographs. Choose one of the photographs and make a list of all the things you can see. Use the ideas to help you.

A B

people

colours

objects

clothes

parts of the vehicle

buildings

2 Answer these questions about your photograph.

1 What type of vehicle is it?
2 What type of street is it?
3 What are the people in the photo doing?
4 Why are they doing it?
5 How do you think they feel about it?

3 Now look at the other photograph and answer these questions.

1 What's the same or similar?
2 What's different?

2 Speaking

1 Which is better, living in a city or living in the country? Why?

**2 Look at the adjectives in the box. Which would you use to describe
a) living in the city? b) living in the country?**

calm	crowded	peaceful	clean	noisy
dirty	boring	relaxing	stressful	convenient
expensive	exciting	safe	lonely	interesting
fun	dangerous	polluted	inconvenient	

**3 Make lists of the advantages of living in a) the city and b) the country.
Use the words in the box to help you.**

shopping	night-life	fresh air	way of life	education
employment	transport	health		entertainment

4 Talk to another student. Decide who is Student A and who is Student B. Use your lists to have a discussion about life in the two places. Use some of the expressions below.

Student A
Try to convince your partner that the city is the best place to live.

Student B
Try to convince your partner that the country is the best place to live.

One big (dis)advantage of the city/country is that...

But we have to remember that it is easier to ...... in the city/country.

Don't forget that the city/country is much more ...... than the country/city.

Another thing is that the city/country is better for...

I'm afraid I don't agree with you because...

Yes, you're right, but I still think...

Get ready for PET Speaking Part 3

1 In Part 3 of the PET Speaking test, you have to talk about a photograph which shows an everyday situation.
2 You have to tell the examiner what you can see in the picture. You talk for less than a minute.

3 Remember:
- start immediately, and keep talking – don't stop and think.
- talk to the examiner, not your partner.
- talk about everything you can see.
- say if you like the photograph or not.
- if you don't know a word, don't stop – talk about something else.
- listen when your partner is talking.

5 When you talk about the photograph, use these ideas to help you.

1 Talk about the *place* in the photograph.
- Is it indoors or outdoors?
- Is it in a house or another building?
- What type of place is it?

2 Talk about the *people* in the photograph.
- How many people are there?
- What do they look like?
- What are they wearing?
- How do they feel?

3 Talk about *what's happening* in the photograph.
- What are the people doing?
- Why are they doing it?

6 Look at the photograph of some people in the countryside. Talk about it using the ideas in 5.

7 Look at the photograph of people in a city and talk about it. Remember:
- don't talk for more than one minute
- talk about everything you can see in the picture
- don't worry about words you don't know

8 Talk about a city you know. Say what you like about it and what you don't like about it.

Food and drink

1 Vocabulary

1 Look at the foods in the box. Divide them into the four groups.

carrots	beans	lamb	peas	onions	garlic
mushrooms	bananas	sausages	grapes	tomatoes	oranges
duck	pasta	beef	rice	chicken	leeks
olives	mayonnaise	tuna	butter	cheese	spinach
pepper	salt	steak	pizza	plums	burgers

Meat and fish	Vegetables	Fruit	Other

2 Add your favourite foods to the lists.

2 Speaking

1 Choose one of the photographs of people eating and talk about it. Remember to talk about everything you can see, including:
- each person – what they are doing, wearing and feeling
- the food and drink
- other things in the foreground
- things in the background

A

B

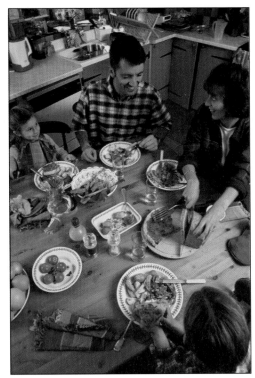

2   **What is your favourite food? Talk about:**
- breakfast
- dinner
- a snack
- a special meal
- a special treat

What do you drink with these foods?

Get ready for PET Speaking Part 4

1 In Part 4 of the PET Speaking test, you have a conversation with your partner. You only have a few minutes for the task.

2 The examiner tells you what to talk about, but does not ask you any questions.

3 The topic of Part 4 is the same as the one in the pictures in Part 3.

4 Remember:
- talk to your partner, not to the examiner
- ask your partner questions
- listen and respond to what your partner says
- don't talk for too long, and give your partner a chance to speak.

 3   **Look at the photographs again and listen to the examiner's instructions for the Part 4 task. What is the topic of the conversation? Make a list of the things you can talk about and the questions you can ask your partner. Think about how to begin the conversation.**

Have the conversation with another student.

 4   **Listen to two students beginning the task. As you listen, think about:**
- how they begin
- how long each person speaks for
- how they show interest in what each other says

5   **Work with another student and do this Part 4 task. Don't talk for too long without involving your partner! Remember to ask questions and show interest. Use some of these phrases.**

That's
interesting
because...

I like ...... ,
don't you?

I agree with you
about that.

Really?

So do I!

Me too,
and another
thing is...

What
about you?

Talk together about good restaurants you have been to and what you like to eat there.

3 Vocabulary

1 **Look at the picture. Can you complete the gaps in this list of ingredients?**

some different-sized .... a hard-boiled ....
a small tin of .... some black ....
two spoonfuls of .... two spoonfuls of ....

What equipment do you think you need to make this recipe?

Now listen and check your ideas.

2 **How do you think you make this recipe? Use these verbs and the ingredients above to talk about it.**

cut	mix	stir
pour	take out	

First you have to...   *Then you...*   *Finally you...*

Now listen and check your ideas. Complete the table as you listen.

	Equipment	Verb	Ingredients
1			
2			
3			
4			
5			
6			
7			

4 Grammar

Finish the second sentence so that it means the same as the first.
1 In our house, the salad is usually prepared by my brother.
In our house, my brother usually ....
2 At breakfast, all the orange juice was drunk.
At breakfast, someone ....
3 My mother told me not to burn the rice.
My mother said, 'Don't ....
4 In the restaurant, Robbie asked for a burger with chips.
In the restaurant, Robbie said, 'Can ....
5 Martine suggested we ordered a pizza.
Martine said, 'Let's ....

Your own space

1 Speaking

Talk about how important each of these things is for you at home:
1   a room or space which is your own
2   a quiet place where you can relax or study
3   a place where you can make as much noise as you like
4   a place where you can invite your friends in comfort
5   your own special seat at the dining table
6   somewhere outside, for example a balcony or garden

2 Reading

1   **Read this text about teenagers. Choose the correct word, A, B, C or D, for each space.**

P E R S O N A L   S P A C E

More and more people live in large cities these days and this means that it is becoming more and more difficult to find space and time for ourselves. But for many people, personal privacy is very important. In many homes, a few minutes in the bathroom is all the privacy that is **(1)** ....

Teenagers especially need their own personal space at home where they can feel relaxed and private. But, of course, not all teenagers are **(2)** .... enough to have a room of their own. Where space is short, they often have to **(3)** .... a bedroom with a brother or sister. In that case, it's a good **(4)** .... for them to have a special area or corner of the room to **(5)** .... their own. It's especially important for young people to have somewhere to **(6)** .... their personal things. This may or may not be a tidy place and it is not a good idea for parents to try and tell teenagers how to **(7)** .... their space as this is **(8)** .... to lead to arguments. Parents can, however, **(9)** .... sure that there are enough storage spaces such as shelves, cupboards and boxes. This will **(10)** .... the teenager to keep their space tidy if they want to.

1	**A** confident	**B** available	**C** general	**D** average
2	**A** dizzy	**B** early	**C** lucky	**D** happy
3	**A** separate	**B** share	**C** divide	**D** join
4	**A** sense	**B** opinion	**C** idea	**D** thought
5	**A** mind	**B** call	**C** say	**D** tell
6	**A** belong	**B** save	**C** support	**D** keep
7	**A** organize	**B** repair	**C** operate	**D** review
8	**A** really	**B** quickly	**C** actually	**D** likely
9	**A** find	**B** make	**C** get	**D** put
10	**A** afford	**B** let	**C** allow	**D** set

2 **Read the complete text again and answer these questions.**

1 What is the writer trying to do in this text?
A complain about something
B blame someone for something
C give advice about something
D warn people about something

2 What does the writer believe?
A Teenagers can be selfish.
B Everybody needs some privacy.
C Parents can be unreasonable.
D Sharing is more important than privacy.

3 What does the writer think about tidiness?
A It is important for teenagers to be tidy.
B It is possible even when space is limited.
C It's a waste of time trying to be tidy.
D Parents should make their children be tidy.

3 Listening

Get ready for PET Listening Part 4

1 Part 4 of the PET Listening test is always a conversation between two people. They will be giving their opinions about something, and agreeing or disagreeing with each other.
2 Remember to read the instructions carefully to find out:
• who is talking
• where they are
• what they are talking about.
This will help you to imagine the situation and understand what they say.

3 Remember to read the statements on the question paper carefully to:
• make sure you know whose opinion the statement is about
• check if the statement matches the text or not.
4 You may not understand all the words in the text. Don't worry, you only have to answer six questions with YES or NO. If you're not sure, guess. You have a 50 per cent chance of being right!

1 **Read the instructions for this Part 4 task.**
• Look at the six statements for this part.
• You will hear a conversation between a man, Bob, and a woman, Mary. They are talking about their teenage children.
• Decide if you think each statement is correct or incorrect.
• If you think it is correct, put a tick (✓) in the box under **A** for **YES**. If you think it is incorrect, put a tick (✓) in the box under **B** for **NO**.

2 **Now listen and complete the task.**

	A YES	B NO
1 Mary's house is too small for Matthew to have his own room.	☐	☐
2 Matthew is a lot younger than his brother.	☐	☐
3 Bob wanted to spend more time alone as a teenager.	☐	☐
4 Matthew would like to have his own computer.	☐	☐
5 Mary feels that Matthew's brother has more need of a computer.	☐	☐
6 Matthew would like to watch the television more.	☐	☐

4 Speaking

What do you think?
1 How do you organize your personal space?
2 Do people respect your personal space?
3 Do you respect other people's space?
4 Do you think that tidiness is important?

5 Listening

Now do this task.
- Look at the six statements.
- Alice and Harry are talking about their personal space.
- As you listen, decide if each statement is correct or incorrect.
- If you think it is correct, put a tick (✓) in the box under **A** for **YES**. If you think it is incorrect, put a tick (✓) in the box under **B** for **NO**.

	A YES	B No
1 Alice regrets arguing with her mother.	☐	☐
2 Alice thinks her mother should put clothes away for her.	☐	☐
3 Alice tidies her room when she's expecting visitors.	☐	☐
4 Alice's wardrobe is too small for all her clothes.	☐	☐
5 Harry sometimes lets his brother wear his clothes.	☐	☐
6 Harry and his brother have to share a bedroom.	☐	☐

6 Speaking

Look at the two photographs. Talk about what you can see in each room.

A

B

Close to nature

1 Vocabulary

Use the words in the box to complete this text about the environment.
Write one word in each space.

breathe	destroying	dusty	fuels	inhabitants	minerals
poverty	prevent	rescue	rubbish	spoil	urgent

STOP DAMAGING THE EARTH!

We have spent the last one hundred years **(1)** .... our environment. In cities, factories and cars pollute the air we **(2)** .... , and everything we touch is **(3)** .... and dirty. We **(4)** .... the countryside by throwing away our **(5)** .... there, and ruin areas of natural beauty by digging up **(6)** .... , such as iron and gold, and **(7)** .... , such as coal and oil. While some people get rich, others suffer from **(8)** .... , hunger and disease. We must **(9)** .... this situation from getting worse. Finding a way to **(10)** .... our planet is an extremely **(11)** .... problem for all the **(12)** .... of the world.

2 Listening

1 Last Saturday three people went out for the day. They each took a photograph.

A   B   C

Listen to the three people talking about the weather on their day out and decide which photo each person took.

Speaker 1 ....   Speaker 2 ....   Speaker 3 ....

2 Listen to the three speakers again and write down all the weather words they use.

Good weather	Bad weather	Other weather words
fine	*storms*	*forecast*

3 Speaking

Talk about:
* weather that makes you feel cheerful/depressed
* clothes you wear in different kinds of weather
* activities you do in different kinds of weather
* the weather and holidays, celebrations and sports events

4 **Reading**

Read this text about giraffes. Choose the correct word, A, B, C or D, for each space.

THE GIRAFFE

Giraffes are the tallest of all animals. When it is born, a baby giraffe **(1)** .... about 1.7 metres and it grows to 5.3 metres in height. The giraffe has a strong and **(2)** .... long tongue (40 cm) which it uses to **(3)** .... leaves off trees. A giraffe **(4)** .... most of the water it needs from leaves and so it can go for more than a month **(5)** .... drinking. When it has a drink, it has to stand with its front legs wide apart in order to **(6)** .... the water. If it needs to **(7)** .... itself, it does so by kicking, but it has **(8)** .... enemies. A lion may jump on a giraffe if one passes under the tree **(9)** .... the lion is sitting, but giraffes have such good eyesight they usually **(10)** .... the lion in time.

1	**A** measures	**B** weighs	**C** looks	**D** appears
2	**A** greatly	**B** much	**C** extremely	**D** too
3	**A** put	**B** carry	**C** bring	**D** tear
4	**A** holds	**B** gets	**C** picks	**D** keeps
5	**A** except	**B** until	**C** through	**D** without
6	**A** reach	**B** arrive	**C** come	**D** move
7	**A** fight	**B** defend	**C** strike	**D** attack
8	**A** little	**B** any	**C** few	**D** other
9	**A** which	**B** where	**C** how	**D** that
10	**A** notice	**B** realize	**C** mind	**D** watch

Get ready for PET Reading Part 5

1 First read through the whole text to get a good idea of the general meaning.

2 Sometimes your knowledge of *vocabulary* is tested, for example in 4. Only one of these verbs (*holds, gets, picks, keeps*) makes sense in this sentence. Try each one in the space before you decide which is the correct word.

3 Sometimes your knowledge of *grammar* is tested, for example in 8. Only one of these words (*little, any, few, other*) is correct here. Which one? Why are the other words incorrect?

4 Sometimes your knowledge of *vocabulary and grammar* is tested, for example in 6. The four words (*reach, arrive, come, move*) have similar meanings but only one is correct here. Which one? If you put *arrive, come* or *move* in the space, what other words would you need to make the sentence correct?

5 Listening 🎧

You will hear someone talking on the radio about some animals and the extraordinary things that happened to them. Put a tick [✔] against the correct answer for each question.

1 How far did Daisy, the cow, fly on her first flight?
A across the road
B across a field
C 2 km
D 5 km

2 What kind of transport does Speedy, the cat, use?
A motorbike
B car
C bus
D bicycle

3 Who finally caught Fluffy, the cat, in the plane?
A the pilot
B a flight attendant
C a passenger
D her owner

4 When does Tom worry about his pigeon, Pete?
A when he's going fast
B when cars are overtaking
C when he's on long journeys
D when he's turning right

5 What did Rambo, the gorilla, do when the boy cried?
A He held his hand.
B He touched his face.
C He put his arm round him.
D He made noises.

6 What had happened to the boy before Prince, the dog, found him?
A He was buried by snow.
B He had fallen down a mountain.
C He couldn't get out of a river.
D He had fallen out of a tree.

6 Speaking

Discuss these questions.
1 Someone wants to give you an animal as a pet. Which one will you choose? Why?

goldfish	kitten	duck	rabbit	mouse	monkey

2 Which of these animals do you think helps humans most? Why?

bee	chicken	cow	elephant	horse	dog

3 Which of these animals would you be most afraid to meet? Why?

spider	snake	shark	bat	tiger	bear

8 2 The wide world

1 Reading

1 Would you like to tour a foreign country on a bicycle? Which countries do you think it would be good to visit in this way? Would tourists enjoy travelling through your country by bike?

2 Read the statements about cycling in Sri Lanka. Then read the text and decide if each statement is correct or incorrect.

1 More people in Sri Lanka ride a mountain bike than any other kind of bike.
2 The writer says that you can go a satisfactory distance each day on a bike.
3 The writer says a bicycle is a restful way of travelling through Sri Lanka.
4 The canals provide water for rice growing in spaces in the jungle.
5 The writer admired the colours of the countryside.

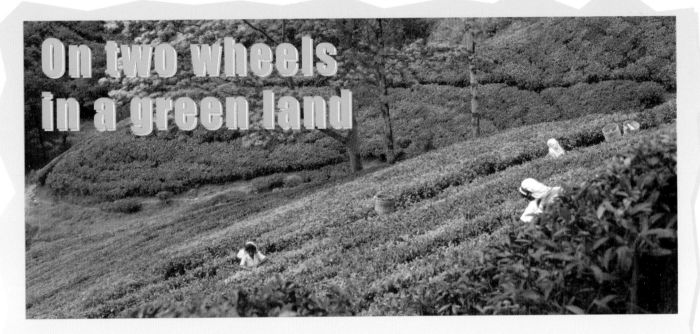

On two wheels in a green land

It is often said that the best way to see a country is to use the method of transport which is traditional in that particular place. So people should see Argentina on horseback, Nepal on foot and the US by car. If this is true, then a bicycle is the perfect way to visit Sri Lanka. Although the 18-speed mountain bike I used is not an everyday sight, more traditional models are popular all over the country.

Sharing the same kind of transport as local people changes the way you see the place. You are travelling at a speed that somehow fits the scenery – not so slow that you only see a small area each day, and not so fast that the details of the countryside are missed. Better still, you can stop whenever you want to listen to the birds or a waterfall, talk to people, smell their cooking or take a photo. However, this doesn't mean cycling in Sri Lanka is relaxing. If you want to see the whole country, you have to leave the towns and villages and cycle through jungle,

where the temperature is 37 degrees, cross streams, climb hills and go over paths which are made of mud, rock or sand.

The most pleasant paths in the jungle follow the irrigation canals. These carry water into the bright green rice fields which appear at regular intervals among the trees. During the afternoon, groups of children, farm workers and water buffalo all come to swim in the canals. Then, when you climb from the jungle up into the hilly area in the centre of the country, you see every hillside is covered with neat rows of tea bushes in another brilliant shade of green. In fact, the whole country is covered in more different and beautiful shades of green than I ever thought possible.

Now I'm wondering where to ride my bike next – perhaps alongside the canals of The Netherlands, or through the city streets of China...

2 Vocabulary

Look at these groups of words. Which one is different?
Example:

sea   ocean   bush   lake
bush *is different because it's not water.*

1 mountain   desert   cliff   hill
2 waterfall   country   continent   district
3 forest   wood   jungle   island   ,
4 stream   canal   cave   river
5 bay   mud   sand   soil
6 path   road   track   wave
7 valley   coast   shore   beach
8 border   flood   frontier   edge

3 Speaking

Do you like adventure films? What difficulties and dangers do the heroes meet?
Who do you want to win in this kind of film – the heroes or the villains?
Imagine this situation.

• A famous director of adventure films wants your advice about the location of his
  next film. Here are some places where the action in the film may happen.

• Talk about the adventures the hero and heroine may have in each place
  and say which you think will be the most exciting.
• Which actors would you like to star in this film? Do you think it would be a
  popular film?

4 Grammar

1 Finish the second sentence so that it means the same as the first.

1 Britain is an island, so everywhere is near to the sea.
Britain is an island, so nowhere is ....

2 Never walk across the desert without taking water with you.
Take water with you if ....

3 Look at a map of the Indian Ocean if you want to find Sri Lanka.
You won't find Sri Lanka unless ....

4 I became a geography teacher five years ago.
I have taught ....

5 The geography teacher asked the students if they wanted to watch a video.
The geography teacher said to the students, 'Would ....

2 Now rewrite these sentences about a family going to live in a different country. Finish the second sentence so that it means the same as the first.

1 Yesterday, our passport photos were taken by a photographer.
Yesterday, a photographer ....

2 My suitcases are heavier than my brother's.
My brother's suitcases aren't ....

3 At first, we'll have great difficulty understanding the language.
At first, understanding the language will be very..

4 We have to find a flat before we can look for a school.
We can't look for a school until we ....

5 My brother and I have both promised to send e-mails to our friends.
I've promised to send e-mails to my friends and so..

Get ready for PET Writing Part 1

1 This part is a test of your grammar. Everything you write must be correct, but don't worry because you only have to write a few words.

2 The second sentence *must* have the same meaning as the first sentence.

3 There are several different kinds of changes that you have to make, but they aren't difficult. For example, sometimes you have to:
- find words with the opposite meaning. (See 1.1 above.)
- change the order of the words. (See 1.2 above.)
- change the tense of the verb. (See 1.4 above.)
- change reported speech to direct speech. (See 1.5 above.)
- make a passive sentence into an active one. (See 2.1 above.)
- change the way you compare two things. (See 2.2 above.)

4 Remember to copy any words from the first sentence very carefully! For example in 1.2 above, did you copy *across the desert* correctly?

Free time

9 1

1 Vocabulary

1 Rearrange these letters to make the names of sports.
Example:
TALLBOFO = football

1 FRIWGUSNNID
2 BLATTNIESEN
3 FLOG
4 STYGNIMCAS

5 DOJU
6 COKYEH
7 SEALLABB

2 Which of these sports do you like playing? What equipment do you need?
Which of these sports do you like watching? What skills must the players have?

2 Reading

What do you like to do in your school holidays?
- These people are all looking for a school holiday activity.
- Read the descriptions of eight school holiday activities on page 55.
- Decide which activity (letters **A–H**) would be most suitable for each person (numbers **1–5**).

1 Gwen is 18 and wants to take her younger brothers and sisters, aged between eight and 15, somewhere where they can get close to animals. She's just failed her driving test.

2 Matthew would like to take his daughter somewhere special on her sixth birthday, but he's only free in the afternoon. She loves hearing stories about animals but is frightened of real ones.

3 Lindsey has 11-year-old twin boys who hate sitting still. She wants to take them somewhere they can enjoy themselves safely all day while she goes to work.

4 Lewis is 15 and wants to do something exciting for the day with some friends from the school swimming team. They're keen to do something connected with either music or sport.

5 Jenny's going to look after her grandchildren, aged ten and seven, for the day. She can't afford to spend any money, but she'd like them to have some entertainment before she takes them home for lunch.

Holiday Fun
for Young People

A Pineapple Theatre Every day at 3 o'clock, young children (4–7 years) can watch 'Stardog'. The fun dog from space invents things to help earth people. At 5 o'clock, a group of 10–16-year-olds presents 'Football Fever', a play about young sports stars. All tickets £3.

B Queen's Arts Centre A day-long course for children (9–13 years) introduces the art of telling stories through music and poetry. Use your own history to make a musical piece. Younger children (4–8 years) may use rubbish to make musical instruments and then play them. No charge for entrance.

C Museum Gardens Circus skills workshop for children (7–11 years). Try juggling, rope walking and putting on clown make-up. Or watch Tiptop Theatre tell the story of a Native American boy and his horse. Both programmes 10–12 am. Entrance free.

D Sunshine Safari We have three floors of slides, swings, rope bridges and other adventure activities. Young adventurers can join a tiger hunt or swim with crocodiles. It all seems very real! Leave your children (3–14 years) in the care of our trained staff. £35 per day, lunch extra.

E Balloon flight See the countryside without having to drive! Our gas-filled balloon is tied to the ground and doesn't actually travel, but the views are fantastic. Price: £12 adult, £7.50 child. No under 5s, no children under 16 without an adult.

F Sea Life Centre Discover facts about life under the sea and watch many varieties of fish. The three-hour tour includes handling starfish, feeding sharks and swimming with dolphins. Adults £4.95, children £3.50.

G Making waves This adventurous programme for 12–18-year-olds gives you a chance to try your skills in a sailing boat, a canoe and a motor boat for just £12 a day. Full instruction is given. You must be a good swimmer and agree to follow all safety rules.

H Paradise Animal Park Drive your car through the park and get close to some of the world's most beautiful and dangerous animals. Younger visitors can have fun in the play area, while there is excitement for older children in the adventure playground with its 10-metre free-fall slide. Family ticket £25.

Get ready for PET Reading paper

1. You have 1 hour and 30 minutes for the Reading and Writing paper. Plan your time carefully.
2. There are five reading parts to the paper. Each part has a different kind of reading text with its own questions.
3. You can get 35 marks for the Reading paper, one mark for each question.
4. In the exam you get a question paper and an answer sheet (see p.92-3). You can make notes on the question paper but you must mark all your answers on the answer sheet.
5. You must use pencil on the answer sheet. Take a pencil, pencil sharpener and rubber to the exam.
6. Read the texts carefully but don't worry if there are words you don't understand. You probably don't need to know them to answer the questions.
7. Mark one letter for each question. To make a change, rub it out carefully and mark the new answer clearly.
8. If there is a question you can't answer, leave it and go back to it later.
9. Near the end of the test time, check your answers and make sure you have marked an answer for everything. If you don't know something, guess – you may be right!
10. There is more information about this paper in the **Get ready** boxes in this book. Make sure you read them again before the exam.

3 | Vocabulary

1 These people are all planning to do their favourite free-time activity. What does each person need? Choose the words from the box.

I'm going to make a skirt to wear to the party tomorrow.

I'm going to decorate my bedroom and put up some shelves.

I'm going to answer this letter from my penfriend.

I'm going to do some work in the garden.

I'm going to have a game of tennis.

1   **2**   **3**   **4**   **5**

balls	brush	dictionary	envelope	flower pot	net
hammer	material	nails	needle	notepaper	
racket	paint	scissors	pins	watering can	
seeds	spade	sports bag	stamp	refreshing drink	

2 What's your favourite free-time activity? What do you need to do it?

4 | Speaking

A friend of yours has just moved to a different town and wants to take up a hobby that will help him/her make new friends. Here are some pictures of some hobbies he/she could do.

- Talk about how interesting the different hobbies are, and decide which will be best for making friends.

Get well soon!

9.2

1 | **Writing**

1 **Do you think you have a healthy lifestyle? What makes your lifestyle healthy or unhealthy?**

2 **Answer the questions on the healthy lifestyle survey.**

> ## Healthy Lifestyle Survey
>
> Modern Living Magazine, PO Box 101, Leeds, UK
>
> Do people today lead healthy lives? Please answer our questions.
>
> Full name: **(1)** ....
> Age: **(2)** ....
> Sex: **(3)** ....
> Height (in metres): **(4)** ....
> Weight (in kilos): **(5)** ....
> How many hours do you sleep each night? **(6)** ....
> What kind of exercise do you do regularly? **(7)** ....
> What did you have for breakfast today? **(8)** ....
> What unhealthy habit do you have which you should give up?
> **(9)** ....
> When you feel under stress, how do you relax?
> **(10)** ....

Compare your answers with some other students. Who do you think has the **healthiest lifestyle?**

2 | **Vocabulary**

Read the sentences about health and sickness and find the missing words in the word square. They are written from top to bottom, left to right, right to left and diagonally.

1 This is an _ _ _ _ _ _ _ _ _ ! Some people have been hurt in a road _ _ _ _ _ _ _ _ , and they need an _ _ _ _ _ _ _ _ _ to take them to hospital.
2 I have bad _ _ _ _ _ _ _ so the doctor sent me to the ear _ _ _ _ _ _ at the hospital. Now I have to take a _ _ _ _ three times a day to make the _ _ _ _ go away.
3 A _ _ _ _ person can't hear without the help of a hearing aid.
4 A doctor and a _ _ _ _ _ both work in a hospital. A _ _ _ _ _ _ _ is a sick person they look after.
5 Even if we had a _ _ _ _ to cure every disease, would everyone be _ _ _ and healthy?
6 Doctor, I feel really _ _ _ . I've got a cold, a _ _ _ _ throat, and a high temperature. And just listen to my horrible _ _ _ _ _ ! I think I've got _ _ _ .
7 When I cut myself with a bread knife, the _ _ _ _ _ was quite deep. There was a lot of blood so my face went _ _ _ _ , I felt _ _ _ _ _ and thought I was going to fall over, but fortunately I didn't _ _ _ _ _ .

A	M	B	U	L	A	N	C	E
C	L	I	N	I	C	U	P	M
C	S	E	H	C	A	R	A	E
I	O	Q	P	J	P	S	T	R
D	R	U	G	I	A	E	I	G
E	E	K	G	F	L	U	E	E
N	I	A	P	H	E	L	N	N
T	T	I	F	A	I	N	T	C
W	O	U	N	D	I	Z	Z	Y

3 Reading

Read the text and questions. For each question, decide which is the correct answer, A, B, C or D.

T V

I'm sure I'm not the only person my age (15) who hates going to the dentist. Channel 4's late-night documentary *Open wide* last Tuesday was excellent for people like me. However, none of my school friends watched it because they didn't know it was on. Why can't television companies let us know about such important programmes in advance?

This programme was important because it showed how methods for helping people with toothache have developed over the centuries. If you think visiting the dentist today is an uncomfortable experience, just be grateful you didn't live 200 years ago! Then, the programme told us, the only cure for toothache was removing the tooth. There weren't any dentists, so the person who cut your hair also pulled out your bad teeth, and there was nothing to stop you feeling the pain.

The programme has also completely changed my attitude to looking after my teeth. My parents were always saying to me things like, 'Don't eat too many sweets,' and, 'Brush your teeth after meals,' but I never paid much attention. Now I've seen what damage sugar can do, especially if I don't use a toothbrush regularly, I'm going to change my habits. Many people would benefit from a repeat of this programme.

Sophie Ashley, Oxford

1 Why has Sophie written this letter?
A to complain about the time a television programme was shown
B to ask for more television programmes designed for school children
C to advise people to watch a particular television programme
D to persuade a television company to show a programme again

2 What can a reader find out from this letter?
A how to encourage young people to take care of their teeth
B where to get information about future television programmes
C what kinds of subjects young people enjoy studying at school
D which television channel shows the most interesting programmes

3 What did *Open wide* say about toothache?
A In the past, nobody could make it stop.
B Dentists used to help people who had it.
C Hairdressers have it more than other people.
D Ways of curing it have changed.

4 What does Sophie think about her parents now?
A They don't know as much as her about teeth.
B Their advice is worth listening to.
C They eat things which are bad for them.
D They don't clean their teeth often enough.

5 Which of these gives information about the programme Sophie watched?

A
11.30 pm *Open wide*
A play about a 19th-century dentist and how he brought comfort to his patients.

B
11.30 pm *Open wide*
The series about health care for teenagers. This week, good eating habits.

C
11.30 pm *Open wide*
This history of the dentist's profession shows what happens when we eat.

D
11.30 pm *Open wide*
How to prepare young children for that first visit to the doctor or dentist.

4 Grammar

Finish the second sentence so that it means the same as the first.

1 I took an aspirin to stop my head aching.
   I took an aspirin because my ....

2 My brother goes jogging because he must keep fit.
   My brother goes jogging to ....

3 If you don't give up coffee, you'll never sleep well.
   You'll never sleep well unless ....

4 People with flu should stay in bed for a few days.
   Stay in bed for a few days if you ....

5 Smoking isn't allowed in hospitals.
   In hospitals, you can't ....

5 Writing

Write this letter to an English-speaking friend.

• You have flu and the doctor has told you to stay in bed for a few days.
• Tell your friend how you feel now, describe how you are passing the time while you are sick, and say what you plan to do when you feel better again.
• Write about 100 words.

Dear Alex,
I've got flu and I have to stay in bed until I'm better. ....
....

Get ready for PET Writing paper

1 You have 1 hour and 30 minutes for the Reading and Writing paper. The writing comes at the end of the paper so plan your time carefully.

2 There are three writing parts to the paper: completing sentences, filling in a form and writing a letter.

3 You can get 25 marks for the Writing paper: 5 marks for Part 1, 10 marks for Part 2 and 10 marks for Part 3.

4 In the exam you get a question paper and an answer sheet (see p.92-3). You can make notes on the question paper but you must write your answers on the answer sheet.

5 Write clearly. You don't want to lose marks because the examiner can't read your writing!

6 When you do Part 1, make sure that you don't make any copying mistakes.

7 You can get a lot of marks for Part 2, so do it carefully! You should only write short answers of 1–5 words.

8 When you write your letter in Part 3, make sure you follow all the instructions.

9 Near the end of the test time, check your answers.

10 There is more information about this paper in the **Get ready** boxes in this book. Make sure you read them again before the exam.

Entertainment

1 How often do you do these things?

watch television	sometimes
go to the cinema	quite often
surf the Internet	not very often
go to a concert	occasionally
go to the theatre	very often
go clubbing	never

2 Match the things in this box with the different types of entertainment.

curtain	encore	website	commercial
interval	soap opera	programme	backing group
ticket	channel	soloist	chat room

3 Say what you like and dislike about each type of entertainment.

1 Complete the text with words from the box. Use each word only once.

part	clap	reviews	rehearsal	screen	camera
performance	series	director	stage	studio	lines

An Actor speaks

As an actor, I much prefer working in the theatre to working on a film or a television **(1)** .... When I get a **(2)** .... in a play, I spend a long time learning my **(3)** .... and then there is a long period of **(4)** .... with the other actors before the first night. The good thing about a play, however, is that you are standing up on the **(5)** .... with a real live audience just a few metres away from you. At the end of the play, if they have enjoyed it, the people all **(6)** .... and you really feel good. It's interesting to read the **(7)** .... in the newspaper, but it's the people who are there who really matter. Working in film or television, however, you spend too much time waiting in the **(8)** .... while the **(9)** .... crew make all the technical arrangements. You sometimes have to do the same bit over and over again until the **(10)** .... is satisfied with your **(11)** .... Then it is months or even years before the film or programme appears on the **(12)** .... By then, you've forgotten all about it and you're in the middle of doing the next thing, anyway.

2 Choose the best answer, A, B, C, or D.

1 Why does the actor prefer working in the theatre?
A You have lots of time to practise.
B It's the same every night.
C There is a live audience.
D He always gets good reviews.

2 What does the actor dislike about working on films?
A It can be boring.
B You can get lonely.
C It is easy to forget your lines.
D You have to do two things at once.

3 Fill in the missing word in these sentences.

1 A .... is someone who writes in a magazine or newspaper.
2 A guitarist is someone who .... a guitar, often in a group.

4 Make similar sentences to explain what these people do.

drummer	director	photographer	TV presenter
disc jockey	comedian	pianist	film critic
interviewer	dancer	singer	violinist

3 Listening

1 Listen to two friends discussing what to do this evening. Where do they decide to go?

A ☐   B ☐   C ☐   D ☐

2 Listen to two friends talking about films. Which type of film do they decide to go and see?

A ☐   B ☐   C ☐   D ☐

3 Listen to two friends discussing a film they have each seen. What did they like most about the film?

A the plot
B the actors
C the characters
D the camera work

4 Speaking

Talk about a film, play or TV programme you have seen recently. Say what was good and bad about it. Remember to include information about the plot, characters and actors.

5 Listening 🔲 Get ready for PET Listening paper

1 You have about 30 minutes for the Listening paper.

2 There are four parts to the paper: Part 1 has seven short texts, Parts 2, 3, and 4 have one long text each.

3 You can get 25 marks for the Listening paper, one for each question.

4 There are pauses between the listening texts. Make sure you use this time to read the questions for the next part, so you are ready to answer.

5 You hear each listening text twice. Answer the questions during the first listening. Check your answers when you hear the text for the second time.

6 In the exam you get a question paper and an answer sheet (see p.92-3). As you listen, write your answers on the question paper. At the end of the test, you have extra time to copy your answers on to the answer sheet.

7 You must use pencil on the answer sheet. Take a pencil, pencil sharpener and rubber to the exam.

8 Copy your answers carefully on to the answer sheet. Mark only one letter for each question. If you make a mistake, rub it out carefully and mark the new answer clearly.

9 Listen carefully, but don't worry if there are words you don't understand. You probably don't need to know them to answer the questions.

10 If there is a question you can't answer, just leave it and move on to the next one. You will probably hear the answer the second time you listen.

11 If you don't know the answer after the two listenings, guess – you may be right!

12 There is more information about this paper in the **Get ready** boxes in this book. Make sure you read them again before the exam.

Now try this listening task. Listen twice, as in the exam.
- Look at the notes about radio programmes.
- Some information is missing.
- You will hear an announcement about the programmes.
- For each question, fill in the missing information.

THIS MORNING'S RADIO

08.00	News
	Arts Review programme
(1)......	– information about theatre, concerts and films
	– special guest: Kevin Jones, (2) .... in a pop band.
08.45	(3) .... with Graham Smith.
08.50	New series: Polly Brown talks to people about (4) ....
09.30	(5) .... with James Grant.
10.15	Radio play called (6) ' .... '

6 Writing

Write a letter to your English-speaking penfriend about a concert, play or film you have been to recently.
- Say where it was, who you went with, and what it was like.
- Write about 100 words.

Dear Tom,
I went to see ....
....

1 **Speaking**

1 **Look at these ways of keeping in touch with people.**

| letters | mobile phone | e-mail | fax | pager |

Talk about:
- how often you use each one
- what you use each one for
- the good and bad things about each one

2 **Look at these two photographs. They both show people keeping in touch with their friends. Choose one of the photographs and talk about it. Remember to talk about all the things you can see, what the people are doing, and how you think they are feeling.**

A

B

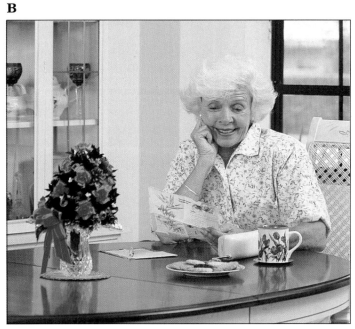

Get ready for PET Speaking paper

1 You have 10–12 minutes for the Speaking paper.

2 You take the test with another student who is your partner. There are two examiners: one tells you what to do and the other one listens. Remember to speak clearly so both examiners can hear you.

3 There are four parts to the paper: talking about yourself, a situation, a photograph, and discussing a wider theme.

4 You can get 25 marks for the Speaking paper. You get marks for how well you communicate with your partner and for your pronunciation. There are also some marks for grammar and vocabulary.

5 Listen carefully to the examiner's instructions. If you are not sure what to do, ask the examiner to repeat them.

6 In Parts 1, 2 and 4, talk to your partner – not the examiner.

7 In Parts 2 and 3 the pictures are there to help you. Talk about what you can see and don't stop after you have talked about one thing. If you can't remember the word for something, don't worry. You can describe the thing or talk about something else.

8 Try to make the test easier for your partner and the examiner by being relaxed and friendly. Remember to ask your partner questions, show an interest in what they say, and give them a chance to speak.

9 There is more information about this paper in the **Get ready** boxes in this book. Make sure you read them again before the exam.

3 **Practise this Part 2 task with a friend. Remember to talk about *all* the pictures, and don't decide too soon!**

The examiner says:

I'm going to describe a situation to you. A friend is going away to study in another town. She will be living on her own in a student flat. She has some money to spend on one piece of electrical equipment, but she doesn't know what to buy. Talk together about the different things she can buy, and then say which will be best.

4 In the Speaking test you have to read out your candidate number. Practise reading out these numbers:

1 61225 0143   **2** 43189 9876   **3** 90906 5539

5 You will be asked to spell a word in Part 1 of the test. Spell these things:

1 your family name
2 your first name
3 the street/district/city where you live
4 the country you come from
5 the name of the school where you study

2 Reading

Read the text below and choose the correct word, A, B, C or D, for each space.

THE RECIPE FOR GOOD COMMUNICATION

How many people do you communicate with in a day? Probably a lot more
(1) .... you did ten years ago. With a few pieces of equipment, we can 'talk' to people in more and more ways, not **(2)** .... face-to-face and on the phone, but also via the Internet. It is very important, therefore, **(3)** .... everyone to try and improve their communication skills. Despite all the technological advances of **(4)** .... years, the art of good conversation is still at the heart of successful communication. **(5)** .... it's a good idea to remember the four golden rules of good communication. Firstly, be as clear as you can. Misunderstandings arise if we don't say exactly **(6)** .... we mean. Secondly, we have to work **(7)** .... at listening. Pay attention to what the other person is saying. Thirdly, ask **(8)** .... people what they think, don't only tell them what you think. And finally show respect for other people, give them time to say what they want, and **(9)** .... interest in what they say.
If you **(10)** .... these rules, you will be a good communicator.

1	**A** like	**B** than	**C** as	**D** that
2	**A** yet	**B** even	**C** just	**D** still
3	**A** for	**B** if	**C** by	**D** from
4	**A** close	**B** last	**C** late	**D** recent
5	**A** There	**B** So	**C** Such	**D** Or
6	**A** when	**B** what	**C** which	**D** whom
7	**A** hard	**B** much	**C** great	**D** very
8	**A** every	**B** other	**C** each	**D** another
9	**A** get	**B** put	**C** be	**D** show
10	**A** act	**B** move	**C** follow	**D** go

3 Grammar

Finish the second sentence so that it means the same as the first.

1 My parents prefer using the telephone to using e-mail.
My parents think using the telephone ....

2 My neighbour is confused by modern technology.
Modern technology ....

3 Whose is this mobile phone?
Who does ....

4 When I look at a screen for too long, I find it tiring.
When I look at a screen for too long, I get ....

5 E-mail makes contacting people a lot easier.
With e-mail, it is ....

PAPER 1 Reading and Writing Test 1 hour 30 minutes

READING

PART 1

Questions 1–5

- Look at the sign in each question.
- Someone asks you what it means.
- Mark the letter next to the correct explanation – **A**, **B**, **C** or **D** – **on your answer sheet.**

Example:

0

> THESE ANIMALS ARE
> DANGEROUS.
> DO NOT CROSS THE
> SAFETY FENCE.

A Don't get any nearer to these animals because they may hurt you.

B Don't let these animals get out from behind this fence.

C It's dangerous to bring animals into this area.

D Only cross the road with animals when it's safe to do so.

Example answer:

Part 1

0 A B C D

1

> *Guided tours of the cathedral tower every hour on the hour*

A It takes over an hour to tour the cathedral tower.

B Meet the guide an hour before the cathedral tower tour begins.

C You'll have to wait an hour for the next tour of the cathedral tower.

D A guide shows visitors round the cathedral tower once an hour.

2

> PASSENGERS MUST NOT CROSS THE RAILWAY LINE UNLESS WITH A MEMBER OF STAFF

A You can walk across the line if a railway worker is with you.

B Railway staff will direct passengers to the way across the line.

C Passengers are never allowed to walk across the line.

D Members of staff should prevent anyone from crossing the line.

3

> The lift telephone is for use <u>ONLY</u> in an emergency.

A If you want to use this telephone, lift the receiver.

B Don't make ordinary calls from the lift telephone.

C All emergencies will be reported on this phone.

D Don't use the lift if there isn't an emergency .

4

> PUBLIC FOOTPATH
>
> Please shut the gate behind you

A When the gate is shut, this path isn't open to the public.

B People should walk one behind the other on this path.

C You may walk here but you shouldn't leave the gate open.

D If you want to walk here, use the gate behind you.

5

> Patients with an appointment should check in at reception before entering the waiting room

A If the waiting room is full, make an appointment at reception.

B You may have to wait for your appointment, so please be patient.

C You could miss your appointment if you leave the waiting room.

D Don't go in the waiting room without informing the receptionist of your arrival.

Guided walks

A This 10-kilometre walk goes along the river valley and up into the hills, where there are wonderful views of the countryside and opportunities to watch birds as they fly south for the winter. Some paths are steep and can get muddy after rain. 8 am start; bring your own lunch.

B We leave at sunset to walk through the woods and look for birds and animals that come out after dark. Bring a torch or candle in a jar. The walk ends two hours later with refreshments in the village where the children's writer Mary Tandy has lived for many years.

C This leisurely walk (three hours) is led by a well-known local history professor. He will show you where the Romans first landed in this country, describe how the port grew in the 17th century, and take you round the historic castle.

D This short walk takes you along the beach where you can look at sea life which has been left behind in rock pools. Bring a net and container if you have them. Starting times (morning, afternoon or evening) depend on the movement of the sea. Please check in advance.

E Take an easy walk through the fields and woods of the little-known Silver River Valley, which is rich in wild flowers. Sorry, no picking! Your guide will inform you about plans to keep this area free from building development and tell you what you can do to help. Mornings only, three hours.

F Discover the wildlife and history of the coast area by walking along the cliff-top path with a knowledgeable guide. This may be done as one long walk (seven hours) or, if you prefer something less tiring, the same ground can be covered on three shorter afternoon walks.

G A fun walk with beach games, beginning at 3 pm. Look for hidden treasure among the rocks and win a prize. Children under 12 must be with a responsible adult. Walkers may also take part in the great beach clean-up. We supply rubbish bags and gloves.

H This walk is for early risers. Watch the sun come up over the hills and listen to the birds' morning song. Walk the short distance to Pirate's Cliff for a breakfast barbecue overlooking the beach. Here, stories from the past about sailors and their ships lost at sea are brought to life by local actors.

PART 2

Questions 6–10

- The people below all want to go on a guided walk.
- On the next page, there are eight descriptions of guided walks.
- Decide which walk (**letters A–H**) would be the most suitable for each person (**numbers 6–10**).
- For each of these numbers mark the correct letter **on your answer sheet.**

Example answer:

Part 2

0	A	B	C	D	E	F	G	H
	▬	☐	☐	☐	☐	☐	☐	☐

6 Julia has three children under 12. They all like short walks, which always make them feel hungry and keen to stop for a snack. Julia wants to encourage the children's interest in nature and history.

7 Russell wants a morning walk which will give him the chance to find something to bring back to show his biology teacher. He has to complete some work about the seashore for her.

8 Harry likes to go on long walks along paths which less serious walkers may find difficult. He's interested in the birds and plants you can find beside rivers.

9 Marcia feels that the natural environment is in danger and likes the idea of a walk which encourages people to care for nature. She enjoys studying different varieties of wild plants.

10 Isabel is looking for a walk in the countryside she can do after studying all day. She'd like to have the opportunity to have something to eat or drink with the other walkers.

PART 3

Questions 11–20

- Look at the statements below about a student photography competition.
- Read the text on the next page to decide if each statement is correct or incorrect.
- If it is correct, mark **A** on your answer sheet.
- If it is not correct, mark **B** on your answer sheet.

Example answer:

Part 3

0	A	B
	■	

11 For the competition, you should take a photograph which shows your opinion of student life.

12 The prizes for the winner include the opportunity to work for a time on a newspaper.

13 Members of the public will be able to see the winner's work.

14 There are over 100 additional prizes.

15 You can enter the competition if you are at least 14 and a student.

16 Each photographer must enter three different pictures for the competition.

17 Everyone should send an envelope with their pictures so they can be sent back.

18 You should make sure your photographs reach the judges by 1st October.

19 FEO will pay for parents to accompany winners if they are too young to travel alone.

20 Photographers will receive money for any of their pictures used in *The Daily Times*.

STUDENT PHOTOGRAPHY COMPETITION

Here's some exciting news. *The Daily Times* newspaper, together with the Further Education Organization (FEO) and The Photographers' Circle, announces a competition for young photographers.

The subject of the competition is 'modern students'. We want your pictures to tell us what it is like to be a student today. Perhaps you think students have a very comfortable life. Or you may believe they have a much harder time at college than former students had. Whatever your feelings, the judges are looking for interesting and original photographs.

The judges will be Ian Scott, the picture editor of *The Daily Times*, Pat Wilton, director of The Photographers' Circle, and FEO's chief executive, Christine Hall.

The first prize winner will get three days of work experience with *The Daily Times* in London, a book worth up to £50 from The Photographers' Circle, and £200 to spend on photographic equipment. *The Daily Times* will print the winning photographs in the newspaper and The Photographers' Circle will include them in an exhibition at their London gallery. The next 12 best photographers will win £100 each to spend on photographic equipment. Their pictures will also be in the FEO's calendar.

Here are the rules:

- The competition is open to students at secondary schools, and at further education, art and technical colleges in England and Wales.
- Students must be on full-time or part-time courses.
- Students must be aged 14 or over on 1st September this year.
- Three copies of each photograph should be sent in and should be no bigger than 25 x 20 cm.
- Up to five photographs may be sent in by one person.
- If photographers want their work returned, they must provide a stamped addressed envelope.
- The competition organizers will take no responsibility for lost or damaged work.
- Photographs that have already been printed in any newspaper or magazine are not acceptable.
- The final date for entries is 1st October this year. Winners will be announced in *The Daily Times* on 17th October.
- A parent or guardian must stay with any winner under the age of 18 while in London. All tickets and accommodation costs will be the responsibility of FEO.
- The judges' decisions are final.
- Photographers must agree to have their pictures printed in FEO publications and *The Daily Times* without payment. The photographer's name will be printed with any picture used in this way.

Send your photographs to:
Photography Competition, PO Box 314, London E17 6LJ.

PART 4

Questions 21–25

- Read the text and questions below.
- For each question, mark the letter next to the correct answer – **A, B, C** or **D** – **on your answer sheet.**

Example answer:

Part 4			
0	**A**	**B**	**C**	**D**
	▬	☐	☐	☐

THE CARPENTER FAMILY

Charles and Alice Carpenter had ten daughters, two sons and numerous grandchildren and great-grandchildren. This makes the Carpenters the perfect subjects for *A Family Century*. The four-part series of programmes shows the family's story from Charles' and Alice's wedding in 1900 to a big family party in 1999.

At first, producer and director Kate O'Driscoll wanted to film a famous family, but she couldn't find a suitable one. 'The older members of famous families were really boring and couldn't remember anything about the past,' she explains. On the other hand, the four remaining Carpenter sisters are excellent storytellers with astonishing memories. The series starts tonight with Madge, Joyce, Sheila and Aline remembering their schooldays in the 1900s. Their father had a good job in the Post Office, but with such a large family there was never enough money. Madge was the only one to go to a good school, which made her look down on her sisters. She calls Joyce 'a pudding', while, in return, Joyce says Madge is 'bossy'.

The women are fascinating, funny and sad, but what makes this series so valuable is the way in which the women's experiences are shown side by side with the social and economic conditions of the day. *A Family Century* is an enjoyable slice of social history which should not be missed.

21 What is the writer trying to do in the text?

- **A** describe the problems of living in a large family
- **B** complain about people who tell boring stories
- **C** explain the importance of studying history
- **D** advise people to watch something on television

22 What can a reader learn about the Carpenter sisters from the text?

- **A** when their parents got married
- **B** how old they are now
- **C** what kind of jobs they did
- **D** how many children they had

23 Why does Madge feel she is better than her sisters?

- **A** She is the oldest.
- **B** She had the best education.
- **C** She has the clearest memory.
- **D** She has the most money.

24 What, in the writer's opinion, makes *A Family Century* valuable?

- **A** It makes you laugh and cry at the same time.
- **B** It gives ordinary people the chance to speak.
- **C** It mixes personal stories with historical fact.
- **D** It isn't afraid to tell the truth about bad times.

25 What did Kate O'Driscoll write when she first contacted the Carpenter family?

A *I'm writing a play about the lives of four sisters who grew up in the 1900s. What can you tell me about life then?*

B *We're looking for families to take part in a television game show. Can you answer questions about history correctly?*

C *I'm making a television series about the social history of the last 100 years. Could people in your family talk to us about their lives?*

D *I'd like to make a television programme about the history of your famous family. Do you have interesting memories of your schooldays?*

PART 5

Questions 26–35

- Read the text below and choose the correct word for each space.
- For each question, mark the letter next to the correct word – **A, B, C** or **D** – on your answer sheet.

Example answer:

Part 5

0	A	B	C	D
	▬	▭	▭	▭

MARY ASTELL

Mary Astell, **(0)** .... was born in 1668, was one of the first people in England to say women **(26)** .... to be educated. As a child, she was **(27)** .... clever that her uncle decided to give her lessons in French, Latin and Mathematics. In 1696, she wrote a book in which she **(28)** .... that a special college for women should be built. Some rich women **(29)** .... her idea and gave her money to start the college. However, important people in the church were against the plan and she never **(30)** .... to do what she wanted. It **(31)** .... another 200 years before the first women's college was built in Cambridge. Mary **(32)** .... on studying and writing her **(33)** .... life. If people **(34)** .... on her door when she was working, she **(35)** .... her head out of the window and said, 'Mrs Astell is not at home.' She died in 1731.

0	**A** who	**B** that	**C** what	**D** which
26	**A** must	**B** ought	**C** can	**D** may
27	**A** such	**B** very	**C** so	**D** too
28	**A** told	**B** offered	**C** suggested	**D** informed
29	**A** supported	**B** agreed	**C** helped	**D** allowed
30	**A** succeeded	**B** could	**C** arrived	**D** managed
31	**A** lasted	**B** took	**C** passed	**D** delayed
32	**A** went	**B** continued	**C** came	**D** brought
33	**A** whole	**B** all	**C** total	**D** full
34	**A** hit	**B** clapped	**C** knocked	**D** struck
35	**A** sent	**B** turned	**C** let	**D** put

WRITING

PART 1

Questions 1–5

- Here are some sentences about some new babies.
- For each question, finish the second sentence so that it means the same as the first.
- The second sentence is started for you. **Write only the missing words on your answer sheet.**
- You may use this page for any rough work.

Example: In our family, we have two new babies.
In our family, there *are two new babies.*

1 The new babies are three months old.
The new babies were born ....

2 The babies' names are Anna and Mark.
The babies are ....

3 Anna drinks more milk than Mark.
Mark doesn't drink ....

4 The babies have received many presents from friends and relations.
Friends and relations have ....

5 Anna and Mark both sleep a lot.
Anna sleeps a lot and so ....

PART 2

Questions 6–15

- An international magazine wants to find out about its readers' clothes-buying habits.
- You have agreed to complete the magazine's questionnaire.
- Look at the questionnaire and answer each question.
- **Write your answers on your answer sheet.**
- You may use this page for any rough work.

QUESTIONNAIRE

FASHION TODAY
27 Eastern Way, Swindon SD3 4KL, UK

Full name: (6) ....
Home address (including country): (7) ....
....
Date of birth (day/month/year): (8) ....
Sex: (9) ....
Occupation: (10) ....
What clothes (one thing) have you bought most recently?
(11) ....
How much did it cost? (12) ....
How often do you buy shoes? (13) ....
Who goes with you when you buy clothes? (14) ....
What colour do you wear most often? (15) ....

Thank you for answering our questions.

PART 3

Question 16

- You have just spent the evening in an English-speaking friend's house.
- Now you are writing a letter to thank this friend.
- Tell your friend what you particularly enjoyed about the evening, invite your friend to spend an evening in your home next week, and say what you plan to do then.
- **Finish the letter on your answer sheet, using about 100 words.**

Dear . . . . . . ,
Thank you for the wonderful evening I had in your house. . . . .
. . . .

You must write your answer on
the separate answer sheet

PAPER 2 Listening Test about 30 minutes

PART 1

Questions 1–7

- There are seven questions in this Part.
- For each question there are four pictures and a short recording.
- You will hear each recording twice.
- For each question, look at the pictures and listen to the recording.
- Choose the correct picture and put a tick (✓) in the box below it.

Example: What's the time?

3 Where does the boy find his keys?

A ☐   B ☐   C ☐   D ☐

4 What present are they going to buy?

A ☐   B ☐   C ☐   D ☐

5 What is today's soup made from?

A ☐   B ☐   C ☐   D ☐

6 Which instrument is Lucy playing these days?

A ☐   B ☐   C ☐   D ☐

7 How will John travel to London?

A ☐   B ☐   C ☐   D ☐

1 Which bus goes to the harbour?

A ☐   B ☐   C ☐   D ☐

2 What can you see at the festival every day?

A ☐   B ☐   C ☐   D ☐

PART 2

Questions 8–13

- Look at the questions for this Part.
- You will hear a woman talking about her work.
- Put a tick (✔) in the correct box for each question.

8 In her first job, Kathy worked as

- **A** ☐ an economist.
- **B** ☐ a salesperson.
- **C** ☐ a flight attendant.
- **D** ☐ a travel agent.

9 Why did Kathy first go to China?

- **A** ☐ on holiday
- **B** ☐ to start a business
- **C** ☐ as part of her job
- **D** ☐ to buy some things

10 What problem did Kathy have on her second trip to China?

- **A** ☐ She had too little money to buy the silk.
- **B** ☐ She couldn't find the people who sold the silk.
- **C** ☐ She wasn't able to buy a small amount of silk.
- **D** ☐ She had problems transporting the silk.

11 When Kathy started her business in London

- **A** ☐ she only made shirts.
- **B** ☐ she worked in her own home.
- **C** ☐ she continued working for the airline.
- **D** ☐ she made all the clothes herself.

12 Why are Kathy's clothes so popular?

- **A** ☐ They are all made in China.
- **B** ☐ They are all made out of silk.
- **C** ☐ They are not like other clothes.
- **D** ☐ They are designed for famous people.

13 How is Kathy's business changing?

- **A** ☐ She doesn't only make clothes these days.
- **B** ☐ She is not using Chinese silk anymore.
- **C** ☐ She is making clothes out of cheaper materials.
- **D** ☐ She doesn't design the clothes herself anymore.

PART 3

Questions 14–19

- Look at the information about a holiday in Australia.
- Some information is missing.
- You will hear a man talking about his holiday.
- For each question, fill in the missing information in the numbered spaces.

HOLIDAY IN AUSTRALIA

Name of the island: **(14)** ....

Best way to get there: By **(15)** ....

Number of rooms in the hotel: **(16)** ....

Activities available at the Kids' Club:

- collecting shells
- **(17)** ....
- watersports
- concert for parents

Activities available to all visitors:

- **(18)** ....
- deep-sea diving
- studying local wildlife

Things to buy on the island:

- work by local **(19)** ....
- T-shirts and baseball caps

PART 4

Questions 20–25

- Look at the six statements for this Part.
- You will hear a conversation between two teenage friends, Tom, a boy, and Sally, a girl.
- Decide if you think each statement is correct or incorrect.
- If you think it is correct, put a tick (✓) in the box under **A** for **YES**. If you think it is incorrect, put a tick in the box under **B** for **NO**.

	A YES	B NO
20 Tom finds his mother's attitude difficult to understand.	☐	☐
21 Sally thinks that Tom's mother is being unfair.	☐	☐
22 Tom agrees that his car-cleaning business was unsuccessful.	☐	☐
23 Tom thinks that parents will pay to see the show.	☐	☐
24 Sally is unsure whether the show is a good idea or not.	☐	☐
25 Sally agrees to take part in the show.	☐	☐

PAPER 3   Speaking Test   about 12 minutes

PART 1 (2–3 minutes)

Before the test begins the examiner asks you to read out your candidate number.
In this part of the test you will have to ask your partner questions about personal details,
for example, where he or she lives, goes to school or work, etc. You also have to answer
your partner's questions.
At the end of Part 1 the examiner will ask you to spell a word, for example part of your
name, address etc.

PART 2 (2–3 minutes)

The examiner says:

I'm going to describe a situation to you.
One of the students in your class is leaving to go and live abroad with his/her family.
You would like to give him/her a present on the last day of school. Talk together about
the sorts of presents you can give and then decide which will be best. (See p.77.)

PART 3 (3 minutes)

The examiner says:

Now I'm going to give each of you a photograph of people relaxing. Would you show
it to your partner and talk about it please. (See p.78.)

PART 4 (3 minutes)

The examiner says:

Your photographs both showed people relaxing. Now I'd like you to talk together
about what you do when you want to relax, when you are alone and when you are
with friends.

CANDIDATE MATERIAL – PART 2

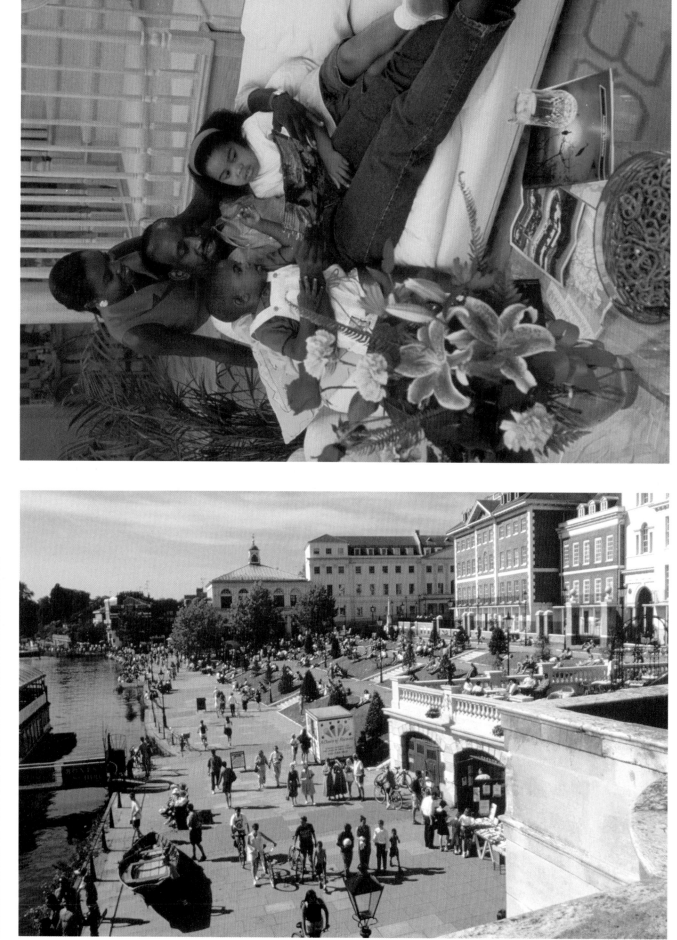

PAPER 1 Reading and Writing Test 1 hour 30 minutes

READING

PART 1

Questions 1–5

- Look at the sign in each question.
- Someone asks you what it means.
- Mark the letter next to the correct explanation – **A, B, C or D – on your answer sheet.**

Example:

0

> THESE ANIMALS ARE DANGEROUS.
> DO NOT CROSS THE SAFETY FENCE.

A Don't get any nearer to these animals because they may hurt you.

B Don't let these animals get out from behind this fence.

C It's dangerous to bring animals into this area.

D Only cross the road with animals when it's safe to do so.

Example answer:

Part 1

0	A	B	C	D
	▬	▭	▭	▭

1

> Offer this seat to old or disabled people, or those carrying young children.

A Young children should offer their seats to anyone older than them.

B If you have children with you, don't let them sit on this seat.

C This seat is mainly for people who find it difficult to stand.

D Help disabled people by offering to carry their children for them.

2

> PLEASE KEEP YOUR PERSONAL PROPERTY AND CLOTHING CLEAR OF THE LIFT DOORS.

A Make sure your things aren't in the way of the lift doors.

B You must wear proper clothes if you want to come in here.

C Don't use this lift for transporting your personal belongings.

D Don't leave any of your things behind when you get out of the lift.

3

> *We cannot allow latecomers to enter until a suitable break in the play.*

A We'll start late so there won't be a break in the play.

B There's a break in the play when you can leave if you want to.

C Some people watching this play may not find it suitable.

D If you're late, you won't be able to go in immediately.

4

> ANY BICYCLE LEFT HERE FOR MORE THAN 14 DAYS WILL BE REMOVED.

A You can't park your bicycle here for longer than two weeks.

B We are holding a sale of bicycles here for the next 14 days.

C For two weeks from today, bicycles should keep to the left on this road.

D This bicycle park will be closed for 14 days.

5

> S P O R T S C E N T R E
>
> Sorry! Gym showers out of order. Use ones by swimming pool.

A We're sorry none of the showers in the sports centre is working.

B After using the gym, you'll have to go somewhere else for a shower.

C The showers are better in the gym than in the swimming pool.

D Book your shower before you use the gym or swimming pool.

PART 2

Questions 6–10

- The people below all want to buy a CD-ROM.
- On the next page there are descriptions of eight CD-ROMs.
- Decide which CD-ROM (letters **A–H**) would be the most suitable for each person (**numbers 6–10**).
- For each of these numbers, mark the correct letter **on your answer sheet.**

Example answer:

Part 2

0	A	B	C	D	E	F	G	H

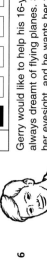

6 Gerry would like to help his 16-year-old daughter who has always dreamed of flying planes. She can't be a pilot because of her eyesight, and he wants her to think about other job possibilities.

7 Erica is looking for a present for her 14-year-old son. He loves listening to all kinds of music, but she'd prefer him to start playing music himself.

8 Paula knows she has a good figure but apart from that she isn't satisfied with the way she looks. She wants something which will help her change her appearance.

9 Daniel got some money for his thirteenth birthday from his grandmother. He really wants to get a racing game, but she says he must buy something which will help him with his school work.

10 Patricia (15) loves speed and even writes poems about it. She can't wait to have driving lessons and would like something which gives her a good idea about being in control of any kind of vehicle.

CD-ROMs

A Magic makeover

Have you ever wanted to see whether a new hairstyle would suit you before you visit the hairdresser's? Now you can experiment with hundreds of hairstyles, glasses and make-up fashions. Both men and women can find the perfect face for themselves with this useful tool.

B Write now

Young people (aged 8–18) can develop their writing skills, creativity and story-telling ability by writing about a very important subject: themselves. They are encouraged to write poems, songs, diaries and stories about their family and friends, things they love and hate, their secret hopes and wishes.

C Take off

This is more than just a game because you really learn how to fly a plane or helicopter. You study a detailed instruction guide and practise on screen with sets of flight instruments from a variety of aircraft. Experience taking off and landing at any one of 3,000 airports worldwide.

D Speedkid

Young people aged 3–15 can explore and discover with these educational games. Difficulty levels can be changed to suit any player. Activities range from maths problems to word games, from drawing to language learning, all based around fun with fast cars, high-speed trains and planes.

E Top notes

This is an enormous library of all types of music from the last 80 years. Watch performances, listen to recordings, look at 9,000 album covers and photos, and read articles on 4,000 artists. You can search by artist's name, type of music, or period.

F Choose right

This is an essential guide to making the right career decision. You complete a detailed questionnaire and it tells you what you're good at, including your social, practical, creative and leadership strengths. It then shows you what further education and career choices are open to you.

G Personal trainer

You tell the 'trainer' details about your weight, height, etc, and it will give you a personal fitness and body-shaping programme. Whether you are male or female, young or old, want something difficult or easy, you will find a series of suitable exercises here which will make you look and feel better.

H Master class

This has 50 hours of instruction and will give you the basic skills needed to play the guitar. All beginners can learn to play their favourite songs. You can practise in private, but very soon you'll be confident enough to perform in public. You could even make it your career!

★★★★★★ WHISTLER, WESTERN CANADA ★★★★★★★

Where standards are higher, and so are the mountains!

In the spectacular Coast Mountains of British Columbia, just 120 km north of Vancouver and the coast, lies the beautiful village of Whistler.

Winter sports

The country round Whistler is considered by many to be the number one ski resort in North America for a number of reasons:

★ It has the largest skiing area on the continent, with more than 200 marked tracks.

★ It has the two steepest skiing mountains in North America: Blackcomb and Whistler.

★ There are five separate mountain bases, all within five minutes of each other and all with high-speed lifts. This means skiers can reach the ski slopes quickly without ever having to queue for a lift.

★ Visitors have the convenience of being able to ski directly to and from their accommodation in Whistler Village.

★ The winter season runs from November to May, with summer skiing and snowboarding continuing until August.

★ There is an average annual snowfall of 9 m, plus snow-making systems.

★ Additional winter activities include ice-skating, snow-shoeing, paragliding and snowmobiling.

Whistler village

After an exciting day on the slopes, visitors can explore this lovely pedestrian-only village. There are many interesting shops and boutiques, and a variety of places for a drink and a snack, or a delicious meal. Those who are still not tired can dance the night away in a nightclub before going back to rest in one of Whistler's many comfortable hotels and inns. There is a choice of accommodation in all price ranges, though most of it is at the top end of the range.

Summer time

Whistler, the number one ski resort in North America, shows how enjoyable summer in the mountains can be.

With four world-class golf courses, Whistler has become popular as a golfing destination. Each course tests the player's skill in a different way, but all have amazing views. The Whistler Golf Club was given a silver medal for its service by *Golf Magazine*. And remember, it may be summer, but it's still the skiing season in Whistler, so you can ski in the morning and have a game of golf in the afternoon.

The view from the top of either Blackcomb or Whistler mountains will take your breath away. You can go on a guided nature walk, or just go up in the lift to enjoy mountaintop dining. Other unforgettable experiences are a horseback ride above the clouds, or, for the adventurous, a high-speed guided bike ride down the mountain.

There are five lakes and numerous rivers in the Whistler valley, so the visitor has many opportunities to fish, swim, windsurf, canoe, or just relax in the sun on a warm, sandy beach.

PART 3

Questions 11–20

- Look at the statements below about Whistler in Western Canada.
- Read the text on the next page to decide if each statement is correct or incorrect.
- If it is correct, mark **A** on your answer sheet.
- If it is not correct, mark **B on your answer sheet.**

Example answer:

Part 3

0	A	B
	■	☐

11   The distance between Whistler and the sea is less than 150 km.

12   The Whistler area is attractive to skiers because there are many steep tracks.

13   Skiers may have to wait five minutes for their turn on a lift.

14   Skiers should take off their skis before entering Whistler village.

15   Plenty of snow falls naturally each year but, if necessary, nature can be helped.

16   You have to go from place to place in Whistler village on foot.

17   There are more cheap hotels than expensive ones in Whistler village.

18   In summer, it's possible to go skiing and play golf on the same day.

19   A guide will show you the best way to cycle to the top of the mountain.

20   In the Whistler area, it's too cold to sunbathe or swim in the lakes.

PRACTICE TEST 2 – READING

PART 4

Questions 21–25

- Read the text and questions below.
- For each question, mark the letter next to the correct answer – **A, B, C** or **D** – on your answer sheet.

Example answer:

Part 4

0	A	B	C	D
	▬	▢	▢	▢

Tania Moffat, 21, works in her parents' clothes shop with her 18-year-old brother, Rufus. This is what she says:

As children, we used to fight a lot. Rufus did things like steal my diary and read out bits at dinner, but now we've put our childhood differences behind us. Of course, we still argue but these days, because we share an interest in fashion and have common aims for the business, our arguments are positive. Rufus and I manage the shop, while our parents design the clothes we sell. We are often photographed wearing the clothes. Rufus loves to wear things that are unusual or shocking and people come into the shop just to see what he's got on that day. He could become a model in the future.

Our parents got married and had me when they were still teenagers and have brought us up in a free way. When I was a schoolgirl, they often suggested I forgot about my homework and went out instead. When I decided to leave school at 16 and come and work in the shop, they supported me. They knew I had a lot to offer the company, and now they say they couldn't manage without Rufus and me. Their attitude means we all enjoy ourselves, both at home and at work.

21 What is Tania trying to do in this text?

- **A** recommend a good place to buy clothes
- **B** show people how to start their own company
- **C** describe what it's like working in her family's business
- **D** encourage young people to leave school and start work

22 What can a reader find out from this text?

- **A** Tania's attitude to marriage
- **B** Tania's opinion of today's fashions
- **C** Tania's ideas about her future
- **D** Tania's feelings about her job

23 What does Tania's father do?

- **A** He's a fashion designer.
- **B** He's a photographer.
- **C** He's manager of a shop.
- **D** He's a model.

24 What does Tania think about her brother?

- **A** He does things just to make her angry.
- **B** He's easier to get on with than before.
- **C** He isn't as serious about his work as her.
- **D** He should pay more attention to his clothes.

25 What would be the best title for this text?

- **A** *How to avoid arguing with your parents*
- **B** *Why working with your brother is a mistake*
- **C** *Successful and happy at work at only 21*
- **D** *The secret diary of a shop assistant*

PART 5

Questions 26–35

- Read the text below and choose the correct word for each space.
- For each question, mark the letter next to the correct word – **A, B, C** or **D** – on **your answer sheet.**

Example answer:

Part 5

0	**A**	**B**	**C**	**D**
	▬	☐	☐	☐

TRAVEL SICKNESS

Everyone loves to **(0)** .... different places and for most of us the journey between places is also exciting. But **(26)** .... people hate travelling in any kind of vehicle because it **(27)** .... them ill. It happens most often when travelling in cars along roads **(28)** .... go up and down a lot or have many bends, or on boats when the sea is **(29)** .... With travel sickness, people feel dizzy and sick and may **(30)** .... their balance, but they usually feel better as **(31)** .... as the vehicle stops moving and they can **(32)** .... out on to firm ground. The **(33)** .... of the sickness is a small problem in the ear. There are pills you can take to **(34)** .... the sickness, but you **(35)** .... to be careful because after taking these you sometimes feel sleepy.

0	**A**	visit	**B**	look	**C**	stay	**D**	drive
26	**A**	another	**B**	any	**C**	some	**D**	one
27	**A**	does	**B**	puts	**C**	turns	**D**	makes
28	**A**	which	**B**	who	**C**	what	**D**	whose
29	**A**	hard	**B**	rough	**C**	sharp	**D**	strong
30	**A**	drop	**B**	lose	**C**	forget	**D**	fail
31	**A**	often	**B**	well	**C**	soon	**D**	quickly
32	**A**	step	**B**	leave	**C**	depart	**D**	change
33	**A**	reason	**B**	purpose	**C**	cause	**D**	birth
34	**A**	defend	**B**	pass	**C**	mend	**D**	prevent
35	**A**	should	**B**	must	**C**	will	**D**	have

WRITING

PART 1

Questions 1–5

- Here are some sentences about a visit to the zoo.
- For each question, finish the second sentence so that it means the same as the first.
- The second sentence is started for you. **Write only the missing words on your answer sheet.**
- You may use this page for any rough work.

Example: Shall we go to the zoo today?
What about ...*going to the zoo today?* ...

1   The tickets to the zoo aren't expensive.
The tickets to the zoo don't ....

2   Richard asked to visit the lions first.
Richard said, 'Can ....

3   You mustn't give food to the animals.
Giving food to the animals ....

4   In this zoo, there are only a few elephants.
In this zoo, there aren't ....

5   This monkey likes talking to people.
This is the monkey which ....

PART 2

Questions 6–15

- You would like to have a penfriend you can write to in English.
- A penfriend agency has sent you an application form to fill in.
- Look at the form and answer each question.
- **Write your answers on your answer sheet.**
- You may use this page for any rough work.

INTERNATIONAL PENFRIENDS AGENCY
16 Linden Avenue, Nottingham NG6 5TH, UK

Application form

Full name: **(6)** ....
Home address (including country): **(7)** ....

Nationality: **(8)** ....
Age last birthday: **(9)** ....
Job (if you are a student, say what subjects you study): **(10)** ....

Hobbies and free-time interests: **(11)** ....
How often will you be able to write to your penfriend?
(12) ....
Which country would you like your penfriend to come from?
(13) ....
How did you hear about our agency? **(14)** ....
Signature: **(15)** ....

PART 3

Question 16

- In your last English lesson, a new teacher taught the class.
- Now you are writing a letter to an English-speaking friend.
- Describe the new teacher, explain what happened in the class, and say how the students felt about it.
- **Finish the letter on your answer sheet, using about 100 words.**

Dear ......,
I want to tell you about my new English teacher. ....
....

You must write your answer on
the separate answer sheet

PAPER 2 Listening Test about 30 minutes

PART 1

Questions 1–7

- There are seven questions in this Part.
- For each question there are four pictures and a short recording.
- You will hear each recording twice.
- For each question, look at the pictures and listen to the recording.
- Choose the correct picture and put a tick (✓) in the box below it.

Example: What's the time?

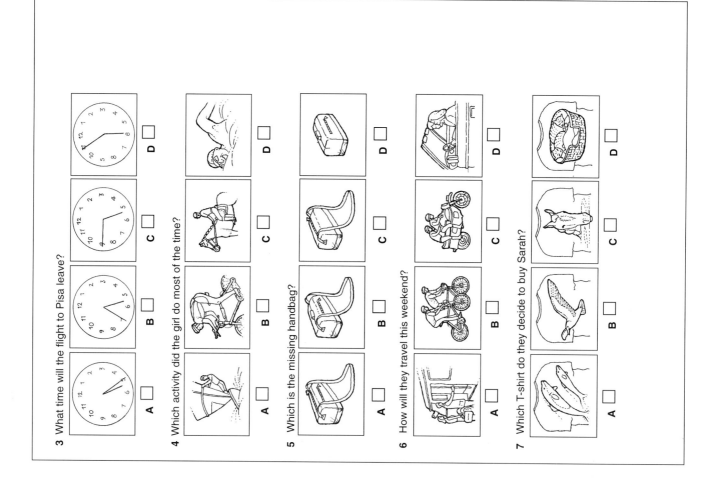

3 What time will the flight to Pisa leave?

4 Which activity did the girl do most of the time?

5 Which is the missing handbag?

6 How will they travel this weekend?

7 Which T-shirt do they decide to buy Sarah?

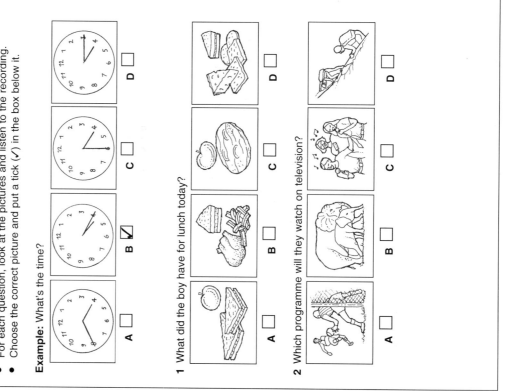

1 What did the boy have for lunch today?

2 Which programme will they watch on television?

PART 2

Questions 8–13

- Look at the questions for this Part.
- You will hear a woman talking about courses at a college.
- Put a tick (✔) in the correct box for each question.

8 A course at the college is suitable for people who

- A ☐ need to study to get a job.
- B ☐ have to pass an examination.
- C ☐ are below a certain age.
- D ☐ want to have fun studying.

9 If you decide to do a course, you have to pay

- A ☐ for each lesson separately.
- B ☐ on a monthly basis.
- C ☐ the whole fee in advance.
- D ☐ a deposit before the first lesson.

10 Which language can you study for the first time this year?

- A ☐ French
- B ☐ Russian
- C ☐ German
- D ☐ Italian

11 Which cookery course is new this year?

- A ☐ basic kitchen skills
- B ☐ advanced cake-making
- C ☐ cooking for special occasions
- D ☐ vegetarian cooking

12 Why can't the college run a course about making pots?

- A ☐ There isn't enough space.
- B ☐ None of the staff can teach it.
- C ☐ They don't have the right equipment.
- D ☐ Not enough people are interested.

13 The new painting course will take place

- A ☐ two days a week.
- B ☐ every day for two weeks.
- C ☐ two afternoons a month.
- D ☐ for two months only.

PART 3

Questions 14–19

- Look at the notes about an artist.
- Some information is missing.
- You will hear the artist talking about his work.
- For each question, fill in the missing information in the numbered space.

PAUL HUNTER: ARTIST

Paul first became interested in drawing when he was **(14)** .... years old.

Paul's first wildlife drawings were of **(15)** .... he saw in the garden.

As a student, Paul did paintings of animals such as **(16)** .... to make money.

The first exhibition of Paul's work was held in a shop which used to sell **(17)** ....

Paul says that his father was a very good **(18)** .... at the exhibition.

People like Paul's paintings because the animals he paints look **(19)** ....

PART 4

Questions 20–25

- Look at the six statements for this Part.
- You will hear a conversation between two teenage friends, Jon, a boy, and Clare, a girl.
- Decide if you think each statement is correct or incorrect.
- If you think it is correct, put a tick (✓) in the box under **A** for **YES**. If you think it is incorrect, put a tick in the box under **B** for **NO**.

		A **YES**	**B** **NO**
20	This was Clare's first holiday in another country.	☐	☐
21	Clare had to understand a foreign language on holiday.	☐	☐
22	Clare enjoyed the lunches she ate on holiday.	☐	☐
23	Jon likes trying foreign food when he's on holiday.	☐	☐
24	Jon thinks Clare's father was right to make her try new things.	☐	☐
25	Clare thinks the last meal of her holiday was the best one.	☐	☐

PAPER 3   Speaking Test   about 12 minutes

PART 1 (2–3 minutes)

Before the test begins the examiner asks you to read out your candidate number.
In this part of the test you will have to ask your partner questions about personal details, for example, where he or she lives, goes to school or work, etc. You also have to answer your partner's questions.
At the end of Part 1 the examiner will ask you to spell a word, for example part of your name, address etc.

PART 2 (2–3 minutes)

The examiner says:

I'm going to describe a situation to you.
A family with young children wants to buy an animal to keep as a pet. Talk together about the types of animals which make good pets and decide which will be best for a family with young children. (See p.90.)

PART 3 (3 minutes)

The examiner says:

Now I'm going to give each of you a photograph of people enjoying themselves.
Would you show it to your partner and talk about it please. (See p.91.)

PART 4 (3 minutes)

The examiner says:

Your photographs both showed people enjoying themselves. Now I'd like you to talk together about what you do when you want to enjoy yourself, when you are at home and when you are on holiday.

CANDIDATE MATERIAL – PART 2

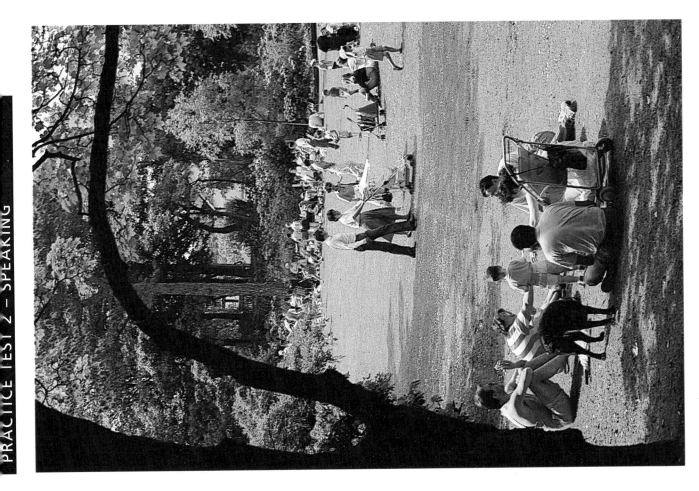

READING AND WRITING – ANSWER SHEET 1

UNIVERSITY of CAMBRIDGE
Local Examinations Syndicate

Candidate Name
If not already printed, write name
in CAPITALS and complete the
Candidate No. grid (in pencil).

Candidate's signature

Examination Title

Centre

Supervisor:
☒ If the candidate is ABSENT or has WITHDRAWN shade here ▭

Centre No.

Candidate No.

Examination Details

PET Reading and Writing Answer Sheet 1

Reading

Use a pencil.

Mark one letter for each question.

Example:
If you think A is the right answer to the question,
mark your answer sheet like this:

| 0 | A B C D |

Rub out any answer you want to change, with an eraser.

Part 1

1	A B C D
2	A B C D
3	A B C D
4	A B C D
5	A B C D

Part 2

6	A B C D E F G H
7	A B C D E F G H
8	A B C D E F G H
9	A B C D E F G H
10	A B C D E F G H

Part 3

11	A B
12	A B
13	A B
14	A B
15	A B
16	A B
17	A B
18	A B
19	A B
20	A B

Part 4

21	A B C D
22	A B C D
23	A B C D
24	A B C D
25	A B C D

Part 5

26	A B C D
27	A B C D
28	A B C D
29	A B C D
30	A B C D
31	A B C D
32	A B C D
33	A B C D
34	A B C D
35	A B C D

Continue on the other side of this sheet →

© UCLES – EFL

READING AND WRITING – ANSWER SHEET 1 (REVERSE)

Writing (Parts 1 and 2)

Write your answer clearly in the space provided.

Part 1: Write your answers below.

		Do not write here
1		1
2		2
3		3
4		4
5		5

Part 2: Write your answers below.

		Do not write here
6		6
7		7
8		8
9		9
10		10
11		11
12		12
13		13
14		14
15		15

Put your answer to Writing Part 3 on Answer Sheet 2 →

© UCLES – EFL

LISTENING – ANSWER SHEET

UNIVERSITY *of* CAMBRIDGE
Local Examinations Syndicate

Centre No.

Candidate Name
If not already printed, write name
in CAPITALS and complete the
Candidate No. grid (in pencil).

Candidate's signature

Candidate No.

Examination Title

Examination Details

Centre

Supervisor:
☒ If the candidate is ABSENT or has WITHDRAWN shade here ▢

SAMPLE

PET Listening Answer Sheet

• You must transfer all your answers from the Listening Question Paper to this answer sheet.

Use a pencil

For Parts 1,2 and 4: Mark one letter for each question.

For example, if you think A is the right answer to the question, mark your answer sheet like this:

| 0 | A |

For Part 3: Write your answers in the spaces next to the numbers (14 – 19) like this:

Change your answer like this:

| 0 | *example* |

Part 1						Part 2						Part 3	
1	A B C D		8	A B C D			14	
2	A B C D		9	A B C D			15	
3	A B C D		10	A B C D			16	
4	A B C D		11	A B C D			17	
5	A B C D		12	A B C D			18	
6	A B C D		13	A B C D			19	
7	A B C D							

Do not write here		Part 4	
14		20	A B
15		21	A B
16		22	A B
17		23	A B
18		24	A B
19		25	A B

READING AND WRITING – ANSWER SHEET 2

Part 3: Write your answer in the box below.

SAMPLE

Do not write below this line

This section for use by SECOND Examiner only

Marks:

Task	0	1	2	3	4	5

Language	0	1	2	3	4	5

Examiner Number

0 1 2 3 4 5 6 7 8 9
0 1 2 3 4 5 6 7 8 9
0 1 2 3 4 5 6 7 8 9
0 1 2 3 4 5 6 7 8 9

Irregular verbs

present	past simple	past perfect
be	was/were	been
beat	beat	beaten
become	became	become
begin	began	begun
bend	bent	bent
bite	bit	bitten
bleed	bled	bled
blow	blew	blown
break	broke	broken
bring	brought	brought
build	built	built
burn	burnt	burnt
buy	bought	bought
catch	caught	caught
choose	chose	chosen
come	came	come
cost	cost	cost
cut	cut	cut
dig	dug	dug
do	did	done
draw	drew	drawn
dream	dreamt	dreamt
drink	drank	drunk
drive	drove	driven
eat	ate	eaten
fall	fell	fallen
feed	fed	fed
feel	felt	felt
fight	fought	fought
find	found	found
fly	flew	flown
forget	forgot	forgotten
forgive	forgave	forgiven
freeze	froze	frozen
get	got	got
give	gave	given
go	went	gone
grow	grew	grown
have	had	had
hear	heard	heard
hide	hid	hidden
hit	hit	hit
hold	held	held
hurt	hurt	hurt
keep	kept	kept
know	knew	known
lay	laid	laid
lead	led	led

present	past simple	past perfect
learn	learnt	learnt
leave	left	left
lend	lent	lent
let	let	let
lie	lay	lain
light	lit	lit
lose	lost	lost
make	made	made
mean	meant	meant
meet	met	met
pay	paid	paid
put	put	put
read	read	read
ride	rode	ridden
ring	rang	rung
rise	rose	risen
run	ran	run
say	said	said
see	saw	seen
sell	sold	sold
send	sent	sent
set	set	set
shake	shook	shaken
shine	shone	shone
shoot	shot	shot
show	showed	shown
shut	shut	shut
sing	sang	sung
sit	sat	sat
sleep	slept	slept
smell	smelt	smelt
speak	spoke	spoken
spell	spelt	spelt
spend	spent	spent
spread	spread	spread
stand	stood	stood
steal	stole	stolen
sweep	swept	swept
swim	swam	swum
take	took	taken
teach	taught	taught
tear	tore	torn
tell	told	told
think	thought	thought
throw	threw	thrown
wake	woke	woken
wear	wore	worn
win	won	won
write	wrote	written

Answer Key

Keys to Units 1–10

1 1 Personal information

2 Listening (page 6)

1

A
Name: John
Surname: Rose
Address: 24 Walton Road, London
Sex: Male
Age: 16
Occupation: Schoolboy
Interests: Football, tennis, volleyball, listening to music, watching television

B
Name: Amanda
Surname: Wilson
Address: 45 Knight Street, York
Sex: Female
Age: 17
Occupation: Shop assistant
Interests: Horse riding, hill walking, getting out of the city

3 Speaking (page 7)

2 1 C   2 E   3 F   4 B   5 G

3 A   D

5 Listening (page 8)

1 Yolanda Brown, 15 White Avenue, Bristol. Telephone: (0117) 791005.
2 Yusuf Amiri, 12 Lincoln Road, Edinburgh. Telephone: (0131) 693210.
3 Angela Beaufort, 16 Chestnut Avenue, Sydney, Australia. Telephone: (00 61 2) 393671.
4 Paolo Mitchell, 243 Upper Park Avenue, New York, USA. Telephone: (00 1 718) 346940.
5 Irina Gallagher, 67 Hollybush Gardens, Gloucester. Telephone: (01452) 332116.

6 Grammar (page 8)

1 a good football player?/good at (playing) football?
2 interested in watersports?
3 old are you?
4 your exact address?
5 spell your surname?

7 Reading (page 8)

1 1 C   2 C

1 2 A regular thing

1 Vocabulary (page 9)

1
attend: class, meeting
boil: water
brush: hair, pet, shoes, teeth
clean: desk, furniture, shoes, teeth
comb: hair
dial: number
dust: desk, furniture
feed: pet
iron: shirt
miss: bus, class, meeting
tidy: desk, dishes, hair
tie: hair, shoelaces
wash: dishes, hair, pet, shirt

2
hand in: books, homework
join in: game
plug in: light, radio
put away: books, game, homework, make-up, socks, umbrella
put on: light, make-up, music, radio, socks
put up: umbrella
take off: make-up, socks
turn on: light, music, radio
turn up: light, music, radio

2 Writing (page 9)

Ralf's answers are not satisfactory for the following reasons:
1 This is not a full name. A full name includes, at least, a first name and a surname.
2 An address will probably include a street name and number, a town and a country.
3 The student should write *German* here, not *Germany*.
4 The day is missing. The name of the month (*july*) should have a capital *J*.
5 This is not an occupation. The answer should be *student*.
6 This is not a sensible answer because there are fewer than 200 hours in a week.

7 This is not a type of programme. If the student never listens to the radio, he should invent a favourite type of programme, eg *music, news*.

8 This is not an answer to the question *Where... ?* If the student never listens to the radio, he should write *nowhere* or invent an answer, eg *in my bedroom*.

9 This is not an activity. If the student listens to the radio in a car, he should write *driving* or *travelling*.

10 This is not a sensible answer because this person is dead and could not give a radio interview! A more sensible answer would be, eg *Leonardo di Caprio* or *André Agassi*.

3 Grammar (page 11)

1 as tidy as yours.
2 faster than Gerry.
3 more comfortable than the new one.
4 less homework than Sally.
5 worse than this (music).

4 Reading (page 11)

2
1 A   **2** B   **3** D   **4** A   **5** C   **6** C   **7** B
8 D   **9** A   **10** B

2 1 You live and learn

2 Speaking (page 12)

2
Her favourite way of studying Spanish is alone.
B is the correct picture.
She likes studying in this way because she's good at grammar, and the book has got lots of practice exercises.

3 Speaking (page 14)

2 **1** F   **2** E   **3** G   **4** C   **5** A
3 B   D

4 Listening (page 14)

1 B   **2** B   **3** A   **4** B   **5** A

5 Grammar (page 14)

1 (for) two hours.
2 much is this CD ROM, please?
3 opinion, a dictionary is very useful.
4 with you about the textbook.
5 talk about the videotape first.

2 2 All the best books

1 Reading (page 15)

a) 2   **b)** 1
a) 1   **b)** 2
1 D   **2** B

2 Vocabulary (page 15)

A travel   **B** romance   **C** humour   **D** mystery
E biography   **F** thriller   **G** horror
H science fiction

3 Reading (page 16)

1 C   **2** E   **3** B   **4** A   **5** G

Get ready box (page 17)

2 C and F
No. A is a novel for teenagers and adults; B is an autobiography for adults; E is a science fiction story for teenagers.
C or F may be suitable. C is for very young children and F is for children between five and ten years old.

3 C is about animals. F is about space travel.

4 F is unsuitable because it is factual and not a story that Laura can read to her grandson many times. The most suitable book is C, because it is for young children and it's about animals.

4 Vocabulary (page 17)

1–5 Answers will vary.

5 Writing (page 17)

Your letter won't be exactly like this, but it should have an apology, an explanantion and an offer.
Model letter:

Dear Lucy,
Something terrible has happened. You remember you lent me 'Rebecca'? Well, I'm afraid it's got very wet. I'm very sorry I didn't look after your book very well.
The book's so exciting I couldn't stop reading it. I was reading it at the bus stop when it started to rain, so I put the book under my jacket. Then the bus came and I slipped as I tried to get on. The book fell out of my jacket, bounced on the pavement and finally landed in a puddle of water.
I know you love this book and I'll buy you a new one as soon as I can. Please forgive me.
Love,
Anna

3 1 Holiday adventures

1 Reading (page 18)

a) 2 **b)** 3 **c)** 1
1 D **2** C **3** A

2 Speaking (page 18)

1
1 a girl
2 in her bedroom
3 packing a suitcase
4 a plastic suitcase, clothes, a quilt
5 excited about her holiday; and nervous, because she doesn't know what will happen.

2
Example:
This picture shows a young woman in her bedroom. She's packing some things in a plastic suitcase, which is on her bed. There are some clothes already in the suitcase and some more on the bed. The bed has a pink-and-white quilt and a pillow on it. I think the young woman is going abroad on holiday so she probably feels excited, but perhaps she also feels nervous because she doesn't know what's going to happen.

Extra details may also be given.
Example:
The young woman has long dark hair and she's wearing jeans and a green T-shirt. The bedroom is quite small and doesn't have much furniture apart from the bed. I think the windows are in the ceiling. There may be a cupboard in the room but I can't quite see.

3
Example:
This picture shows two people in a travel agency. They're...

3 Reading (page 19)

2
1 Incorrect 2 Correct 3 Correct 4 Incorrect
5 Incorrect 6 Correct 7 Incorrect 8 Correct
9 Correct 10 Incorrect

Get ready box (page 20)

2
Statement 4: The Safari Team
Statement 6: Good Food
Statement 9: Quality Camping Equipment
3
Statement 1: *Every seat is a window seat...*

Statement 3: *All safari team leaders... have worked for at least a year...*
Statement 8: *All water carried on the truck is safe... never runs out*
4
No   Yes

4 Grammar (page 20)

1 you have learnt to ski.
2 soon as we arrived at the hotel.
3 the afternoon.
4 was on holiday in Paris.
5 you book your holiday.

5 Vocabulary (page 20)

Transport: car, plane, coach, train
Accommodation: hotel, guest house, tent
Scenery: beach, countryside
Activities: swimming, taking photos, sunbathing, picnics
Things to pack: sunglasses, suntan lotion, guidebook
Souvenirs: postcards, shells, handicrafts

3 2 Just the job

2 Vocabulary (page 21)

1

Profession	Subject studied
architect	architecture
doctor	medicine
lawyer	law
artist	art
cook	cookery/cooking
engineer	engineering
tourist guide	tourism
hairdresser	hairdressing
journalist	journalism
business man/woman	business
actor/actress	acting
chemist	chemistry
biologist	biology
physicist	physics
musician	music

2

Verb	Noun
apply	application
organize	organization
qualify	qualification
decide	decision
operate	operation
employ	employment

advertise   advertisement
govern   government
manage   management
retire   retirement
insure   insurance
succeed   success

3 Listening (page 22)

1

Speaker 1: uniform, car, city centre, controlling traffic.
Speaker 2: jeans, computer, advertising agency, drawing.
Speaker 3: white coat, microscope, zoo, testing.
Speaker 4: suit, phone, bank, helping customers.

1 C   **2** A   **3** D   **4** B

2
1 D **2** B **3** C **4** C **5** A **6** A

4 1 House and home

1 Vocabulary (page 24)

2

Living room: coffee table, armchair, television, lamp, sofa
Kitchen: dishwasher, sink, fridge, cooker
Bathroom: washbasin, shower, towel rail, mirror
Bedroom: wardrobe, chest of drawers, dressing table, television, lamp, mirror

3 Listening (page 25)

1 C

2 C

4 Listening (page 26)

1 C

2 B

3 D

4 C

4 2 Interesting people

1 Vocabulary (page 27)

3

attractive/ugly   careful/careless
cheerful/miserable   confident/shy
foolish/wise   hard-working/lazy
strong/weak

4
amusing/funny   anxious/worried
blond/fair   boring/dull
understanding/patient   honest/truthful
slim/thin
5
Answers will depend on the students.

3 Reading (page 28)

1
1 D **2** C **3** A **4** B **5** C
2
1 C **2** E **3** B **4** D **5** A

4 Grammar (page 29)

1 who is very patient with her students.
2 strong enough to open the classroom door.
3 many students have curly hair.
4 better than serious ones.
5 likes best.

5 1 Places of interest

1 Reading (page 30)

1
1 post office
2 sportscentre
3 hotel
4 giftshop
5 post office
6 museum
7 sportscentre
8 giftshop
9 hotel
10 museum
2
1 c) **2** c) **3** b) **4** a) **5** b)
6 b) **7** a) **8** b) **9** a) **10** a)
3
Example answers:
School:
a) Packed lunches are now available from the canteen.
b) Shoes must not be worn in the hall.
c) The school bus leaves from the main entrance.
Department store:
a) The coffee shop is open on the fifth floor.
b) This lift holds up to five people.
c) Sale begins Friday January 4th.
Bank:
a) New Savings Account 5% per annum.
b) Please wait here until a cashier is free.
c) This branch is open on Saturdays 10.00–13.00.

Airport:
a) Zone A: Check-in for domestic flights
b) Please keep your baggage with you at all times.
c) BA 244 London: Please go to gate 16.

2 Listening (page 31)

1
1   10.00 am
2   £1.20
3   450472

2
1   November
2   6.00 pm
3   old walls
4   museum

3
1   Wednesday
2   leaflet
3   poster

3 Reading (page 32)

1 Incorrect   2 Incorrect   3 Correct   4 Incorrect
5 Correct   6 Incorrect   7 Correct   8 Incorrect
9 Correct   10 Correct

5 2 Getting there

1 Vocabulary (page 33)

1

Taxi: driver, catch, fare, take, meter
Train: driver, catch, miss, get on, ticket, fare, station, take, platform, timetable
Bus/coach: driver, catch, miss, get on, ticket, fare, station, take, timetable
Plane: pilot, attendant, land, catch, miss, get on, take off, check in, ticket, fare, gate, take, boarding pass, timetable

2
1   miss, station
2   catch/take, fare, tickets
3   check in, boarding pass, gate, get on
4   platform, ticket, get on
5   timetable, catch

3 Reading (page 34)

1

A taxi   **B** train   **C** plane
D bus/coach   **E** bus/coach

2   C

3
1 C   2 B   3 D   4 A   5 C

6 1 What a bargain!

2 Reading (page 36)

1   D
2   A
3   C

3 Vocabulary (page 36)

1 earn, save   2 cheque, credit   3 note, coin
4 receipt, owe   5 lend   6 shop   7 charge
8 tip

4 Writing (page 37)

2
1 much   2 you   3 was   4 my   5 fits   6 to
7 with   8 been   9 we   10 to   11 catch/take
12 of   13 the   14 lot   15 an   16 where
17 if   18 can   19 hope   20 send

Andrea says *'Thank you very much… It was kind…'*
She says the sweater *'fits me perfectly'* and *'I love the colour.'* (She says something nice about it.)
She invites Chris by asking a question. *'Have you been… yet? Why don't we…'*
Invitations: *'Please come…', 'I'd really like you to come…', 'Would you like to come…'*
Acceptance: *'I'd love to…'*
Refusal: *'I'm afraid I can't go…'*
Arrangements: *'I could come… your street.'*
Andrea says: *'I hope you can come.'* (an invitation) and *'Phone me or send me an e-mail.'*
Goodbye sentences: *'Please write soon', 'Thank you again…', 'Give my love/best wishes to…', 'See you soon'.*
Hello sentence: *'I'm sorry I haven't… '*
Andrea writes *'Love'* before her signature.
Informal letter: *Best wishes, Yours,*
Formal letter: *Yours sincerely,*

5 Listening (page 38)

1 flowers   2 leather jackets
3 Sunday   4 a hospital

6 2 City life

2 Speaking (page 39)

2

Answers will vary; some words can be used more than once.

a) the city: crowded, noisy, dirty, stressful, convenient, expensive, exciting, lonely, interesting, fun, dangerous, polluted.

b) the country: calm, peaceful, clean, boring, relaxing, safe, lonely, interesting, fun, inconvenient.

3

Some words can be used more than once.

a) the city: shopping, night-life, way of life, education, employment, transport, entertainment.

b) the country: fresh air, way of life, education, health.

7 1 Food and drink

1 Vocabulary (page 42)

1

Meat and fish: lamb, sausages, duck, beef, chicken, tuna, steak, burgers

Vegetables: carrots, beans, peas, onions, garlic, mushrooms, tomatoes, leeks, olives, spinach

Fruit: bananas, grapes, oranges, plums

Other: pasta, rice, mayonnaise, butter, cheese, pepper, salt, pizza

2 Speaking (page 42)

3

The topic of the conversation is food that you eat when you go out and when you stay at home.

3 Vocabulary (page 44)

1

some different-sized tomatoes
a small tin of tuna fish
two spoonfuls of mayonnaise
a hard-boiled egg
some black olives
two spoonfuls of tomato sauce
You need: a mixing bowl, a fork and spoon, and a fairly sharp knife.

2

	Equipment	Verb	Ingredients
1	knife	cut	tomatoes
2	spoon	take out	seeds
3	mixing bowl	put in	tuna and egg
4	fork	mix	tuna and egg
5	spoon	stir in	mayonnaise and tomato sauce
6	spoon	put	mixture into tomatoes
7	knife	cut up	tomatoes and olives

4 Grammar (page 44)

1 prepares the salad.
2 drank all the orange juice.
3 burn the rice.'
4 I have a burger with chips?'
5 order a pizza.'

7 2 Your own space

2 Reading (page 45)

1
1 B   2 C   3 B   4 C   5 B
6 D   7 A   8 D   9 B   10 C

2
1 C   2 B   3 B

3 Listening (page 46)

2
1 A   2 B   3 B   4 A   5 A   6 B

5 Listening (page 47)

1 A   2 B   3 A   4 A   5 B   6 B

8 1 Close to nature

1 Vocabulary (page 48)

1 destroying   2 breathe   3 dusty
4 spoil   5 rubbish   6 minerals
7 fuels   8 poverty   9 prevent
10 rescue   11 urgent   12 inhabitants

2 Listening (page 48)

1

Speaker 1 B   **Speaker 2** C   **Speaker 3** A

2

Good weather: fine, clear, warm, sunshine, hot, sunny, dry up

Bad weather: storms, thunder, lightning, snow, frost, mist, clouds, wind, rain, snow-covered, freezing, foggy, dull, damp, changeable, shower, pouring, cooler, gales

Other weather words: forecast, slipping

4 Reading (page 49)

1 A	**2** C	**3** D	**4** B	**5** D
6 A	**7** B	**8** C	**9** B	**10** A

5 Listening (page 50)

1 C   **2** A   **3** D   **4** B   **5** B   **6** A

8 2 The wide world

1 Reading (page 51)

2
1 Incorrect   **2** Correct   **3** Incorrect
4 Correct   **5** Correct

2 Vocabulary (page 52)

1 *desert* because it's not a word for a high place
2 *waterfall* because it's not an area of land
3 *island* because it doesn't mean a place with a lot of trees
4 *cave* because it's not water
5 *bay* because it's not a kind of earth
6 *wave* because you can't walk down it
7 *valley* because it's not part of the coastline
8 *flood* because it doesn't describe the limit of something

4 Grammar (page 53)

1
1 far from the sea.
2 you (ever) walk across the desert.
3 you look at a map of the Indian Ocean.
4 geography for five years.
5 you like to watch a video?'

2
1 took our passport photos.
2 as/so heavy as mine.
3 difficult (for us).
4 find/have found a flat.
5 has my brother.

9 1 Free time

1 Vocabulary (page 54)

1
1 windsurfing
2 table-tennis
3 golf
4 gymnastics
5 judo
6 hockey
7 baseball

2 Reading (page 54)

1 F   **2** A   **3** D   **4** G   **5** C

3 Vocabulary (page 56)

1
1 material, needle, scissors, pins, refreshing drink
2 brush, hammer, nails, paint, refreshing drink
3 dictionary, envelope, notepaper, stamp, refreshing drink
4 flower pot, watering can, seeds, spade, refreshing drink
5 balls, net, racket, sports bag, refreshing drink

9 2 Get well soon!

2 Vocabulary (page 57)

1 emergency, accident, ambulance
2 earache, clinic, pill, pain
3 deaf
4 nurse, patient
5 drug, fit
6 ill, sore, cough, flu
7 wound, pale, dizzy, faint

3 Reading (page 58)

1 D   **2** A   **3** D.   **4** B   **5** C

4 Grammar (page 59)

1 head was aching/ached.
2 keep fit.
3 you give up (drinking) coffee.
4 have (got) flu.
5 smoke.

10 1 Entertainment

1 Speaking (page 60)

2

curtain: theatre, concert
interval: concert, theatre, cinema
ticket: cinema, concert, theatre, clubbing
encore: concert, theatre
soap opera: television
channel: television
website: the Internet
programme: television, concert, theatre
soloist: concert
commercial: television, cinema
backing group: concert
chat room: the Internet

2 Vocabulary (page 60)

1

1 series   **2** part   **3** lines   **4** rehearsal
5 stage   **6** clap   **7** reviews   **8** studio
9 camera   **10** director   **11** performance
12 screen

2

1 C   **2** A

3

1 journalist   **2** plays

3 Listening (page 61)

1 B

2 D

3 A

5 Listening (page 62)

1 8.15/eight fifteen   **2** drummer
3 weather forecast   **4** wild flowers
5 *The Cookery Programme*   **6** *Happy Times*

10 2 The age of communication

2 Reading (page 65)

1 B   **2** C   **3** A   **4** D   **5** B
6 B   **7** A   **8** B   **9** D   **10** C

3 Grammar (page 65)

1 is better than (using) e-mail.
2 confuses my neighbour.
3 this mobile phone belong to?
4 tired.
5 (much/a lot) easier to contact people.

Key to Practice Test 1

Paper 1 Reading and Writing

page 66 Reading PART 1
1 D   2 A   3 B   4 C   5 D

page 67 Reading PART 2
6 H   7 D   8 A   9 E   10 B

page 68 Reading PART 3
11 A   12 A   13 A   14 B   15 A   16 B
17 B   18 A   19 A   20 B

page 69 Reading PART 4
21 D   22 A   23 B   24 C   25 C

page 70 Reading PART 5
26 B   27 C   28 C   29 A   30 D   31 B
32 A   33 A   34 C   35 D

page 71 Writing PART 1
1   three months ago
2   called/named Anna and Mark
3   as/so much milk as Anna (does)
4   given/sent many presents to the babies or
    given/sent the babies many presents
5   does Mark

page 71 Writing PART 2
6   more than one name should be given, with ini-
    tial capital letters
7   address, including name of country
8   date must be given in order specified
9   male/female
10 any job, eg *student, pupil, unemployed, retired*
11 any item of clothing
12 any price, in any currency
13 any expression of time frequency, eg *every
    month, hardly ever,* etc.
14 any person, eg *my mother, my friend*
15 any colour

page 72 Writing PART 3
Letters are assessed for *task* and for *language* on
two scales of 0–5 (with a possible total mark of 10).
In their letters, students should include the
following three points:

• some remarks about what made the evening at
  the friend's house enjoyable
• a return invitation to the student's home next
  week
• some information about how the evening there
  will be spent

Paper 2 Listening

page 73 Listening PART 1
1 B   2 D   3 C   4 D   5 B   6 B
7 C

page 74 Listening PART 2
8 B   9 C   10 C   11 D   12 C   13 A

page 74 Listening PART 3
14   DUNK
15   plane
16   147 (one hundred and forty-seven)
17   horse riding
18   boat trips
19   artists

page 75 Listening PART 4
20 B   21 A   22 A   23 A   24 A   25 B

Note: The Practice Tests are sample
tests only, and are not actual UCLES
past papers.

Key to Practice Test 2

Paper 1 Reading and Writing

page 79 Reading PART 1
1 C   2 A   3 D   4 A   5 B

page 80 Reading PART 2
6 F   7 H   8 A   9 D   10 C

page 81 Reading PART 3
11 A   12 A   13 B   14 B   15 A   16 A
17 B   18 A   19 B   20 B

page 82 Reading PART 4
21 C   22 D   23 A   24 B   25 C

page 83 Reading PART 5
26 C   27 D   28 A   29 B   30 B   31 C
32 A   33 C   34 D   35 D

page 84 Writing PART 1
1   cost much/a lot (of money)
2   we visit the lions first?'
3   isn't/is not allowed/permitted
4   many/a lot of/lots of/elephants
5   likes talking to people

page 84 Writing PART 2
6   more than one name should be given, with initial capital letters
7   address, including name of country
8   any nationality, in its anglicized form, correctly spelt with initial capital letter
9   any appropriate age, in figures or words
10 any job or subjects of study
11 any hobbies/interests
12 any specific expression of time frequency, eg *every week, once a month*
13 any country, in its anglicized form, correctly spelt with initial capital letter
14 any reasonable source
15 the same name as that in question 6, *not* printed

page 85 Writing PART 3
Letters are assessed for *task* and for *language* on two scales of 0–5 (with a possible total mark of 10). In their letters, students should include the following three points:

* some description of the new teacher
* some information about what took place in the class
* some description of the feelings of the students

Paper 2 Listening

page 86 Listening PART 1
1 B   2 B   3 D   4 B   5 A   6 D   7 A

page 87 Listening PART 2
8 D   9 B   10 B   11 D   12 C   13 A

page 87 Listening PART 3
14   8/eight
15   birds
16   lions and tigers
17   furniture
18   salesman
19   real

page 88 Listening PART 4
20 A   21 B   22 A   23 A   24 B   25 B

Note: The Practice Tests are sample tests only, and are not actual UCLES past papers.

Tapescripts for Units 1–10

1 1 Personal information

2 Listening (page 6)

1

A Hello. My name is John, that's J O H N. And my surname is Rose, that's R O S E. I would like to give you some information about myself. First of all, I live in London and my address is 24, Walton Road. That's Walton W A L T O N, Walton Road in London. So, what else can I tell you? I'm a 16-year-old boy and so I'm still at school and I'm very interested in sport. I'm quite good at football and I also enjoy playing tennis and volleyball. When I'm not playing sport, I like listening to music and watching television.

B Hello. My name's Amanda Wilson and you spell my first name A M A N D A, Amanda and my surname is Wilson, which is spelt W I L S O N. My name's not really difficult to spell, but people always make mistakes in my address. I live in York, that's Y O R K, at 45 Knight Street which is spelt K N I G H T Street. I'm a 17-year-old English girl and I work as a shop assistant in a large shop in my home city. In my free time, I like to get out of the city, however, and I'm very interested in horse riding and hill walking. I'm not very good at horse riding yet because I only started last year, but I've been hill walking since I was 12 years old. I love it.

3 Speaking (page 7)

3

David: Hello. I'm David.

Victoria: Hi. I'm Victoria. I'm a friend of Tom's from college.

David: Yes, I'm one of his friends too, and we play football together. What do you study?

Victoria: I'm doing languages. What about you?

David: I've finished college, actually, and I'm working as a windsurfing instructor.

Victoria: Oh, I'm really interested in watersports, but I'm not very good at windsurfing.

David: That doesn't matter. You could learn.

Victoria: Yes, I suppose so. But what I'm really interested in is sailing.

David: So am I. I'm running a course which starts next week. Would you be interested in joining?

Victoria: Oh... I might be... it depends.

5 Listening (page 8)

1 My name is Yolanda Brown, that's Y O L A N D A B R O W N, 15 White Avenue, that's W H I T E A V E N U E, Bristol, that's B R I S T O L. Telephone: (0117) 791005.

2 My name is Yusuf Amiri, that's Y U S U F A M I R I, 12 Lincoln Road, that's L I N C O L N R O A D, Edinburgh, that's E D I N B U R G H. Telephone: (0131) 693210.

3 My name is Angela Beaufort, that's A N G E L A B E A U F O R T, 16 Chestnut Avenue, that's C H E S T N U T A V E N U E, Sydney, that's S Y D N E Y, Australia, A U S T R A L I A. Telephone: (00 61 2) 393671.

4 My name is Paolo Mitchell, that's P A O L O M I T C H E L L, 243 Upper Park Avenue, that's U P P E R P A R K A V E N U E, New York, that's N E W Y O R K, USA. Telephone: (00 1 718) 346940.

5 My name is Irina Gallagher, that's I R I N A G A L L A G H E R, 67 Hollybush Gardens, that's H O L L Y B U S H G A R D E N S, Gloucester, that's G L O U C E S T E R. Telephone: (01452) 332116.

2 1 You live and learn

2 Speaking (page 12)

2

Boy: Hello, Polly. How are your Spanish classes going?

Polly: Oh, OK. The teacher's very nice, but the classes are a bit boring. I really like studying on my own, you know. My dad bought me a Spanish CD for my computer, but actually I prefer the textbook because I'm good at grammar, and the book has got lots of practice exercises. One day, I'd like to be able to listen and understand the words to Spanish pop music, but I'm not good enough for that yet!

3 Speaking (page 14)

3

Valerie: So, our friend wants to learn a new language?

Pietro: That's right, and he's only got £20 to spend, so he can't buy all these things, can he?

Valerie: No, he can't. Let's start by talking about which of them will be useful for him.

Pietro: OK, then afterwards we can decide which one he should buy.

Valerie: OK. Shall we start with this one, the dictionary?

Pietro: Yes, I think he should buy one of those, because it's very useful if you don't know what words mean.

Valerie: Yes, I agree, and it's also good for checking spelling. But what about a textbook? They're useful too.

Pietro: Yes they are, but maybe he won't need one because he'll have a teacher.

Valerie: Possibly. Or he may get one free when he pays for the course.

Pietro: Oh yes, that's a good point.

4 Listening (page 14)

Tim: Hi Janet. How's your computer course going?

Janet: Oh, I've just had my class, actually. We have them twice a week and each one lasts two hours.

Tim: Gosh. That's long. Doesn't it get boring?

Janet: Well, you need that long to actually do a whole document. It's really good because I can do all sorts of things on my computer that I never even knew existed before.

Tim: I can't say the same for my cookery course.

Janet: Oh, Tim, why not? I thought you were enjoying it.

Tim: Oh it's enjoyable enough, but we just don't seem to make much progress. We spent the whole of last week's lesson learning how to fry an egg.

Janet: Well, it's not an easy thing to do properly, you know.

Tim: Oh I know, but I don't even like eggs.

Janet: Oh poor Tim! So how often is it?

Tim: Just once a week, for an hour and a half.

Janet: And do you get to eat all the things you make?

Tim: Well, you're not meant to eat them there, but you can take them home because you have to buy all the stuff in the first place. It's cakes next week.

Janet: Oh, that sounds fun.

Tim: Oh yes. I'm looking forward to it. But Janet, I wanted to ask you something, actually. Have you learnt how to send e-mails on your course yet?

Janet: Oh yes, we did that in the first week.

Tim: Because I can't get my computer to send them properly, and I was wondering if you'd show me how it's done?

Janet: Well, if you bring me one of your cakes, I suppose I could try.

Tim: Great, well, when I've made them…

3 2 Just the job

3 Listening (page 22)

1

1

I love what I do and I'm very proud of the uniform I wear. I drive around for most of the day but I'm always somewhere in the city centre. My job is controlling the traffic. When I hear there's a traffic problem I go and see what I can do about it. I just use my hands and my voice – no equipment's necessary – except for my car, of course. I couldn't work without that!

2

I never did well at school. I was only interested in drawing – I was quite good at that. And that's what I do now – drawing. I work in an advertising agency and I do the artwork for advertisements. But I don't use a pencil or paint – it's all done on a computer – that's the only piece of equipment I need. I like being comfortable when I work, so I wear jeans. I don't even own a suit.

3

This is my first job and I've only been here for a year. My microscope is my most important piece of equipment. I couldn't do my work here in the zoo without it. I love animals but I don't often get to see the ones here! My job is testing. I test all kinds of things – the animals' food, the water they drink, and if they get ill, I test their blood. It's very important that everything here is clean, so I have to wear a white coat over my clothes, and I'm always washing my hands!

4

Actually, I want to change what I do. I work in a bank, and it's a good job, but I'd like to do something more exciting. Here it's the same thing every day. My job is helping customers. I help customers when they come into the bank and I help them when they phone up. I don't really have any equipment apart from the phone. I spend a lot of time on the phone. I have to wear a suit at work, which I hate – I'd much prefer to wear jeans!

2

Presenter: ...and today in our series about people who work for themselves, we have Amanda Turner. Good morning, Amanda. Tell us what you do.

Amanda: Hi! Well, basically I'm a cook. Unlike most cooks, I'm not employed by a restaurant but by various recording studios. When musicians are making an album, they have to stay in the studio all day, so I go there and prepare meals for them. I used to cook for dinner parties in people's homes but that wasn't as much fun.

Fortunately, people seem to be satisfied with what I do. When they're recording, musicians want something tasty but quite simple. They don't want to eat a lot or be given unfamiliar dishes. The food has to be good for them because they're always worried about getting ill or putting on weight! I do quite a lot of vegetarian food.

Generally, my job isn't stressful. I only get worried when they forget to tell me how many people will want a meal or they tell me to expect five and then it's fifteen! Often I don't have a proper kitchen to work in, and sometimes the meal is ready long before the musicians have finished playing. But I don't mind that. I know I'm lucky to be my own boss, to do work I enjoy, and to get paid well for it! And I meet all sorts of interesting people. Think of your favourite boy band and I've probably cooked them a meal! But I work with all kinds of musicians, pop and classical, famous and unknown, young and old. I'm happiest when I'm cooking for the young ones. They always really enjoy my food and say nice things about it.

I have a long day. I walk round the market every morning buying vegetables, and then I cycle to the place where I get fresh meat and fish. I have to be at the studios by noon. I don't drive, and anyway it's always difficult to park, so they send a car to pick me up. Going on the bus with all my bags of shopping would be terrible! After cooking, serving and clearing up, I never get home before nine in the evening. My daughter prepares a snack for us while I tell her about the day's music. I also do a cookery page for a monthly magazine, so before I go to bed, I do some work on that. I should write a shopping list for next day, but I'm always too tired!

4 1 House and home

3 Listening (page 25)

1

In my room, there's not much furniture. I've got a bed, of course, but I don't have a wardrobe because I keep all my clothes in a chest of drawers. My parents don't like me putting posters on the wall, and for a long time I didn't have any, but I've recently been allowed to put up one or two. My parents bought me a desk to do my homework on, but I don't use it much. I like my room. It's nice.

2

I don't live in the centre of the city, so I live in a house rather than a block of flats. Although the house is on the edge of the city, the buildings are quite close together and we don't have a garden. One day, I would really like to live in a big house a long way away from other people with lots of trees around it, but the house I live in is near to the school, so for the moment it's alright, and I've got some good friends who live in the house next door.

4 Listening (page 26)

1

Boy:	Mum, I can't find my calculator.
Mum:	Isn't it on your bedside table?
Boy:	I've looked there and in the chest of drawers, but it's not there.
Mum:	I saw a lot of things pushed under the bed when I was cleaning yesterday. It's probably there. If not, have you looked in the wardrobe?
Boy:	Oh, it's OK. I've found it on the floor like you said. But I don't understand how it got there!

2

Man:	Excuse me , I've just missed the 3.35 bus. Can you tell me what time the next one leaves?
Woman:	Certainly sir. There's a bus to London at 3.45 and one to Manchester at 4.35.
Man:	Oh. I wanted the London bus, actually. I didn't think it would be so soon.
Woman:	Yes, there's one at 3.45 and then another at 4.45. But there wasn't one at 3.35, that one was going to Edinburgh, so you haven't missed it really.

3

Waiter:	Would you like to order, madam? Today's soup is tomato, or we have some cheese and tomato pizza. The other pizzas are all finished, I'm afraid.
Woman:	Oh, that's a shame. I want more than a sandwich, but I didn't want to eat too much. Umm... OK then, I'll have chicken and chips, please.
Waiter:	I'm sorry, the chicken's finished, but we could do you a burger?
Woman:	Oh, really? In that case I'd rather have a sandwich, just plain cheese, please.

4

Woman:	Hello, I've come to cut Susie's hair for her.
Man:	Oh yes, come in. She's expecting you.
Woman:	I wasn't sure what to bring. I've brought some special shampoo she might like to try, it's very good, and I've got scissors and a comb. But if she wants her hair washed, I might need to borrow something to dry it with, because I'm thinking of blow-drying it.
Man:	Oh... I'm afraid we haven't got a hairdryer, but I can give you a towel if you want.

5 1 Places of interest

2 Listening (page 31)

1

Hello. This is the Orford Castle Information Line. Orford Castle is an 800-year-old building which is located near the sea at Orford in the east of England. The castle opens every day at 10.00 am, and stays open until four o'clock in the afternoon. It takes about one hour to look around the castle and you can climb a spiral staircase to the top of the tower, which is 30 metres high. From there, you can see for miles. Admission prices are as follows: adults £2.30 and children £1.20. Children receive a free Activity Sheet and can find out more about the castle in the interactive CD ROM unit. A full-colour souvenir guide is also available. For more information about Orford Castle, phone 01394 450472 during office hours. Thank you for calling the Orford Castle Information Line.

2

Hello and welcome to the Framlingham Castle Information Line. Framlingham Castle is open between the months of April and November. The castle dates back to the 12th century and from the outside looks much as it did 800 years ago. The castle opens at 10.00 am and closes at 6.00 pm. Once inside the castle, most people walk around the old walls, from where you get a wonderful view of the surrounding countryside, but there are also a number of other things to see and do. There is also a museum to visit, where you can get lots of information about the castle's history, and a fully interactive audio tour is available for adults and children alike. Admission costs £2.95 for adults and £1.50 for children. Thank you for calling the Framlingham Castle Information line.

3

Hello and welcome to the Castle Rising Information Line. Castle Rising is open to the public from Wednesday to Sunday each week at this time of year, opening at 10.00 am and closing at 3.30 in the afternoon. Admission costs £2.30 for adults and £1.70 for children. When you enter the castle, you will be given a free leaflet giving you information about its history, and explaining what you can see as you walk round. It takes about an hour to visit the castle, but if the weather's nice, you can bring a picnic to eat in the park and stay as long as you like. There is a small giftshop at the castle where you can buy a souvenir poster to remind you of your visit. We look forward to seeing you at Castle Rising. Thank you for calling.

6 1 What a bargain!

5 Listening (page 38)

This is Radio London Fun calling all tourists in London! Did you know that East London has some of the most interesting street markets in Europe?

First up, there's Columbia Road market. You can buy flowers here at any one of 50 stalls. And whatever flowers you choose, they won't cost you much!

Next, there's Brick Lane market. Not everything here is new, but there's something for everybody. And if you're looking for a really good souvenir of London, then check out this market's speciality, leather jackets. You'll have to try one on!

Then, there's Petticoat Lane Market, the oldest and most famous of all London's markets. Buy anything here, from fashionable clothes to toys for the children. Come any morning from Monday to Friday, or on Sunday, when the market is at its biggest and most crowded.

Finally, there's Whitechapel market. It's easy to get to because it's right by the underground station, and just across the road from a hospital. This is the place to buy exotic vegetables and spices from Asia.

So, get down to East London now and be part of the fun!

7 1 **Food and drink**

2 Speaking (page 43)

3

Examiner: Your photographs showed people eating a meal. Now I'd like you to talk together about the type of food you eat when you go out and when you stay at home.

4

Examiner: Your photographs showed people eating a meal. Now I'd like you to talk together about the type of food you eat when you go out and when you stay at home.

Girl: So, Tom, do you often eat out?

Tom: Sometimes... sometimes I go out for a meal with my family, and sometimes I go with my friends. What about you?

Girl: Yes, me too. What type of restaurant does your family go to?

Tom: Different types, but usually traditional ones. They like to have steak and chips and things like that, but I prefer Italian food...

Girl: Really! So do I. It's much more interesting than English food, isn't it?

Tom: Yes, I agree with you about that, and another thing is that it isn't very expensive.

Girl: That's right. When I go out with my friends, I always go to either an Italian or a Chinese restaurant.

Tom: Yes, me too... and also Thai... have you tried Thai food?

Girl: No, what's it like?

Tom: Well, it's similar to Chinese, but it has different tastes and unusual vegetables.

Girl: Oh, that sounds good!

Tom: Yes, you should try it.

3 Vocabulary (page 44)

1

I'm going to tell you how to make tomato owls. First of all, you need some different-sized tomatoes, some big ones and some smaller ones, and a small tin of tuna fish. As well as these two main ingredients, you also need two spoonfuls of mayonnaise, a hard-boiled egg, and some black olives. To give colour, you will also need two spoonfuls of tomato sauce.

You don't have to cook the owls, but to make them you do need some basic equipment. Firstly, you need a mixing bowl to make the mixture in. To make the mixture you need a fork and a spoon, and to cut up the tomatoes and olives you need a fairly sharp knife.

2

So, now I'm going to tell you how to make the tomato owls. Firstly, take the knife and cut the tomatoes in half. Then take the spoon and use it to take the seeds out of the middle of the tomatoes, so that there's a hole for the mixture to go in. Then put the tuna and the hard-boiled egg into the mixing bowl. Then, using a fork, mix them together. When you have a good mixture, stir in the mayonnaise and the tomato sauce, using a spoon. Now take some of the mixture on the spoon and put it into the bottom half of each tomato. Cut the remaining tomato pieces into triangles to make the owl's mouth and ears, and cut up an olive to make its eyes.

7 2 Your own space

3 Listening (page 46)

2

Bob: Hello, Mary, how are you?

Mary: Oh, hello Bob. Not too bad. We're having one or two problems with our son Matthew.

Bob: Really? What sort of problems?

Mary: Well, he wants to have his own bedroom, but we haven't got the space and he doesn't seem to understand.

Bob: Oh, so he shares with his brother, does he?

Mary: Yes, but there's not a great age difference, just one year, so you'd think they'd be able to get on together, wouldn't you?

Bob: I remember I used to hate sharing a bedroom with my older brothe. We used to argue all the time. Mostly about privacy, as I remember.

Mary: Privacy? You mean you wanted more time to be alone?

Bob: It wasn't that. It was more that I wanted to have my own space. You know, we had one wardrobe, one chest of drawers. I didn't even have one drawer that was all mine, and so my elder brother used to just take all my things if he fancied them.

Mary: Oh, I see. I wonder if that's Matthew's problem? Because he wanted his own computer, but there's not room for two in the one small bedroom, so we said no, they'd have to share.

Bob: So who gets to use it all the time?

Mary: I don't know, but they always seem to be fighting about something, and of course Matthew doesn't have as much homework as his brother, so maybe he doesn't need it so much.

Bob: Well, they're not only for doing homework on, you know.

Mary: I know that Bob, and they've got their own television in the room, but Matthew doesn't really seem to like television very much. I don't understand him sometimes.

Bob: Well, maybe it's because he doesn't get to watch the programmes he likes.

Mary: Actually, I think he'd rather not have the television in the room. I think I'd better talk to them about these things. Maybe we can arrange things better. Thanks Bob.

Bob: Don't mention it.

5 Listening (page 47)

Alice: Oh, hello Harry, how are you?

Harry: Fine, thanks. But you look a bit miserable. What's the matter?

Alice: I've been arguing with my mum again, I'm afraid. I feel sorry about it afterwards, but she just annoys me *so much*.

Harry: Yeah, I know what you mean. But what have you been arguing about?

Alice: Oh, the usual thing about my bedroom.

Harry: Your bedroom?

Alice: Yeah. She's always telling me to tidy it up, but it's my room, so I don't see why I should have to.

Harry: And is it really untidy, or is it just that she's *really* fussy about things like that?

Alice: Oh, it's untidy all right. I mean, you know, I take my clothes off at night and just leave them where they fall.

Harry: And you expect your mum to tidy up after you?

Alice: No, I do it sooner or later because it's not good for your stuff to be left screwed up in a ball, is it? It's just that she wants it done like *now*, and I'm happy to leave it for a while and do it later, you know, when I feel like it, or when I've got friends coming round.

Harry: And so you argue?

Alice: Yeah. She wants me to put everything back in the wardrobe, but I've got so much stuff that it won't all fit anyway.

Harry: You're lucky. I have to share a wardrobe with my brother. He's always wearing my things without asking me.

Alice: But don't you each have your own bedroom?

Harry: We do, but his is very small and you can't get a wardrobe in, so he's always coming in and out of my room to get stuff out of it.

Alice: Oh, I wouldn't like that.

Harry: Nor do I. It leads to *lots* of arguments.

8 1 Close to nature

2 Listening (page 48)

1

1

I listened to the weather forecast before we set out and it wasn't encouraging – storms with thunder and lightning and even snow on the hills! Actually, it was a fine, clear day. There was frost on the ground when I woke up and some mist over the fields, but that soon disappeared in the warm sunshine. There were some clouds about, but the wind kept them moving and it didn't rain. All in all, it was a brilliant day!

2

It was lucky we didn't have far to walk on Saturday. I couldn't help slipping on the snow-covered pavements and the air was freezing! But, really, I like that kind of weather best. It kind of makes me feel alive – not like foggy days, or dull, damp ones when I just want to stay indoors, or very hot and sunny ones which send me to sleep! So it was a great day!

3

You know what they say about the weather being changeable? Well, it wasn't like that on Saturday! It was one heavy shower after another – just when we thought it was going to dry up, it started pouring again! Still, it was quite warm, though it got cooler in the evening, so we didn't really mind. I heard later there were gales on the coast, so we escaped them! In spite of the weather, we really enjoyed our day!

5 Listening (page 50)

I've collected several extraordinary animal stories, and I'd like to tell you some of them.

One day, Daisy the cow was peacefully eating grass. Suddenly, a very strong wind blew her up into the air and carried her two kilometres, before landing her safely in a neighbour's field. But that wasn't Daisy's only flight. Five years later, passengers in a bus were amazed to watch as another strong wind lifted Daisy into the air, carried her over their heads, and brought her down on the other side of the road.

You think that's strange? Well, what about Speedy, the cat, and her love of travelling fast? Speedy loves riding on the back of her owner's motorbike and overtaking buses and bicycles. Speedy's owner had to stop her riding on the roof of his car, because it's too dangerous, and he makes her wear a special hard hat for protection when she's on the motorbike.

Another extraordinary cat is Fluffy. Once, when Fluffy was a passenger on a plane, she travelled with the luggage but she escaped from her box. The flight attendants tried to catch her and so did the pilot, but without success. Fluffy travelled backwards and forwards between New York and Los Angeles for 12 days before her owner got her to come out for a nice piece of fish.

Then there's Tom Johnson's pet bird, a pigeon called Pete. Tom drives thousands of kilometres a year, and Pete flies with him. He rides on a stream of air beside the right-hand window of the car, which gives him high speed for little effort, a bit like surfing on a wave. Tom gets anxious that other cars might hit Pete when they pass him, but, apart from that, they both enjoy the long journeys.

Now let me tell you about Rambo, the gorilla. Rambo lives in a zoo and one day a little boy somehow fell into the gorillas' cage. He was hurt and couldn't get up. Rambo made noises to stop the other gorillas coming near the boy, and when he cried, he gently dried the boy's tears with his hand. The way he kept the boy safe has made Rambo famous.

And, finally, let me tell you about another animal that rescued a child. Prince, the dog, lived in a forest on a mountain. One day, he found a little boy half-frozen under a deep pile of snow. He used the heat from his body and his warm tongue to unfreeze the child, and then he carried him on his back to the nearest house.

Well, you must agree, animals can be just amazing!

10 1 Entertainment

3 Listening (page 61)

1

Man: What do you feel like doing tonight? I'm getting a bit tired of clubbing.

Woman: Yeah, me too. How about going to the open-air concert? The guitarist is meant to be *really* good.

Man: Oh, I heard that all the tickets were sold out weeks ago, but there's a good film on at the ABC. You know, it's the one that won all the Oscars.

Woman: OK, and if we can't get in, there's always the theatre next door. That's never full, so it's a good idea.

2

Woman: It's *great*, this new cinema! *Four* films on at the same time, and they're all good.

Man: Well, I don't know about that. There's a good thriller on in Screen Number One, or I wouldn't mind seeing the science fiction one, that's meant to be really good.

Woman: Well, I'm not keen on seeing either of those. But how about the one about animals, that's much more my sort of thing than the other one... what is it? Some sort of romantic comedy?

Man: That's right. Oh well, I'm quite happy to go along with your choice.

3

Man: So, what did you think of it?

Woman: Well, he's a brilliant director, isn't he? All those lovely scenes in the mountains... the camerawork was *wonderful*.

Man: I thought the actors were good on the whole, although to be honest, I think the storyline, the plot, is *so* strong that you don't worry so much about the characters. I mean, it is a classic action film, isn't it?

Woman: I *absolutely* agree with you. I was on the edge of my seat the whole time! You never knew what was going to happen next. That's what *really* made it for me.

Man: Oh yeah, me too.

5 Listening (page 62)

It's now five to eight and there's just time for one more song before the news, but before I do that, I'd just like to tell you about one or two things coming up later today on your local radio station.

First of all, after the eight o'clock news, at 8.15, we have our *Arts Review* programme. Debbie Clarke will be telling you about what's on in the region in the coming week, including information about theatre, cinema and concerts. Today Debbie will also have a special guest in the studio, Kevin Jones, who is the drummer with the very successful pop band, *Splodge*. Kevin will be talking about what it's like to be the drummer rather than the lead singer in a pop band.

That's followed at 8.45 by the weather forecast. Graham Smith will be here to tell you if it's going to be wet or fine for the rest of the week. Let's hope that Graham has some good news for us. After that, at 8.50, a new series begins. Polly Brown has been out and about in the countryside this week talking to people who are interested in wild flowers. And I must say that some of those people really know a great deal about the subject.

After that, at 9.30, we have *The Cookery Programme*. James Grant will be back with some more delicious recipes, and he'll also be telling us what to look out for when we're buying fresh fruit and vegetables. And finally, at 10.15, we have this morning's radio play. *Happy Times* it's called, and it tells the story of two children's summer holiday by the seaside and something which happened that was to change their lives forever. Sounds good. So, that's it on your favourite station today. Now up to the news here is *Splodge* with their latest single, which is called *'Take me'*.

Tapescript for Practice Test 1

Practice Test 1 - Paper 2 Listening

page 73 PART 1

RUBRIC = R

R: There are seven questions in this part. For each question there are four pictures and a short recording. For each question, look at the pictures and listen to the recording. Choose the correct picture and put a tick in the box below it.

Before we start, here is an example.

R: What's the time?
Man: Could you tell me the time please?
Woman: Of course. **It's twenty past four.**

R: The woman told the man the time. The second picture is correct and the tick has been put in box B below that picture.

Now we are ready to start. Here is a short recording for the first four pictures. Don't forget to put a tick in one of the boxes! Listen carefully...

R: One: Which bus goes to the harbour?

Girl: Excuse me. Do you know which bus goes to the harbour? Is it the number 24 or the number 27?
Man: Oh, I'm not sure. The 24 used to go to the harbour, but I think they changed the route last year. **I think it must be the 25** because the 26 goes up the hill, away from the sea, and the 27 is the school bus.
Girl: Oh, I see. Thank you.

R: Two: What can you see at the festival every day?

The Denton Arts Festival is taking place between the 12th and 21st of August this year. There is **an exhibition of paintings open daily** and a programme of evening activities which offers something different each day, including cinema, drama, music and dance. The festival concludes with an open-air jazz concert on Saturday evening which will be followed by a display of fireworks. A weekly ticket, which gives entry to all the events, costs as little as £20. For further details and booking information, call the box office on Denton 58982.

R: Three: Where does the boy find his keys?

Boy: Mum, I've lost my keys again. But I must have had them to get in the front door last night.
Mum: Yes, I'm sure I saw them next to the telephone, but they're not there now. Are you sure that they're not in your jacket pocket?
Boy: No, I wasn't wearing one last night because it was raining. I had my raincoat on... Oh, it's alright, I've got them... **I'd left them in the lock.**
Mum: Oh, honestly!

R: Four: What present are they going to buy?

Man: What shall we get Darren and Kylie as a wedding present?
Woman: Well, Kylie's made a list and some people have already chosen things. Aunt Olive is getting them the knives and forks they've asked for, and Darren's mother is getting them a microwave oven. I was thinking of getting either a nice picture to hang on the wall, or some saucepans. What do you think?
Man: Oh, I think **something for the kitchen's much safer than a work of art.** They may not like it.
Woman: OK then. That's agreed.

R: Five: What is today's soup made from?

Woman: Excuse me, on the menu it says 'soup of the day'. I hope it's not boring old tomato soup. I had mushroom soup here once, and it was excellent. Is that on the menu today?
Waiter: The chef does a range of soups, madam. **Today it's chicken,** I'm afraid, although he does make the mushroom one sometimes, and we may have some fish soup if you would prefer it?
Woman: No, the soup of the day will be fine, thanks.

R: Six: Which instrument is Lucy playing these days?

Man: How is Lucy getting on with the violin?
Woman: Oh, we've given it to her cousin. She found it much more difficult to play than the guitar, and so **she's gone back to playing that instead.** She'd like to try the piano next, but they're rather expensive, so she will have to wait a bit until we can afford one. Meanwhile, she's quite happy

because with her brother on drums, they can make quite a lot of noise between them.

Man: I bet.

R: Seven: How will John travel to London?

Woman: Is John driving up to London on Sunday?

Man: **He's taking the coach**, actually. He thought about going by train, but it's too expensive. The plane's actually cheaper than the train these days, but he still can't afford it.

Woman: Well, at least the coach is more relaxing than having to drive in this weather.

Man: That's true.

page 74 PART 2

R: You will hear a woman talking about her work. Put a tick in the correct box for each question.

Kathy: Hello, my name's Kathy Parks and I run my own fashion company in London. I've come to talk to you this evening about my career. After studying economics at college, I got a job **as a salesperson** with a large airline. It was a great job. I didn't travel as much as the pilots and flight attendants, of course, but I did get to see the world without having to pay for expensive holidays.

That was how **I came to go on a marketing trip to China** in 1993. At that time, I hadn't thought about starting my own business, and I had no knowledge of the world of fashion. But while I was shopping one day, I came across some wonderful silk material. I bought some home with me and made it into clothes for myself and friends, just for fun.

My friends liked those clothes so much that I decided to go back to China to try and buy some more of the silk. This time, however, the people who sold it said that they were not able to let me have such a small amount again, and that **they would only sell it in large quantities.** I wasn't sure what to do, but as I had gone all that way, I didn't think I could come home without any material. That was how I came to spend my life's savings on four kilometres of silk.

When I got it back home to London, I gave up my job and started my own business. Working in a friend's garage, I turned that silk into 8,000 silk shirts and 800 silk ties **with my own hands**. Fortunately for me,

they sold very well. And that was the beginning of my fashion business.

I now design and make all sorts of clothes out of silk and other materials and they are very popular. I also draw the patterns that are printed on the material in China before it comes to London. I think my clothes are **quite different from others** you find on the market and that's why all sorts of people notice them in the shops and buy them, even models, film stars and professional people.

My business is growing all the time. **I have now started designing and making handbags and travel goods to match the clothes I make as well**. But I don't want the business to become too large, because I think people like the fact that I design everything myself, and that everything is made from the highest quality materials, much of it still imported from China.

page 74 PART 3

R: Look at the information about a holiday in Australia. Some information is missing. You will hear someone talking about his holiday. For each question, fill in the missing information in the numbered spaces.

Man: Good evening. I've come to talk to you this evening about a small island in Australia which I visited last year. Before we see the video, let me tell you something about the island. It's called **Dunk** island, yes that's **D U N K,** and it's a tiny dot on the map just off the coast of Queensland in north-eastern Australia.

The easiest way to get to the island is to take a plane from the international airport at Cairns on the mainland. The flight takes around 45 minutes, although if you don't like flying, there's also a coach which comes across on the ferry, but this takes over two hours.

Most of the island is covered in rainforest and it's absolutely beautiful. There is only one place to stay, **a hotel which has 147 rooms** and is situated right on the beach. It doesn't look as big as it sounds, because most of the rooms are in small buildings surrounded by trees.

Families are welcome at the hotel, which has a very good 'Kids Club' for 3–14 year-olds. The club has activities such as collecting shells, as well as the more usual **horse riding** and watersports. Every week, what's more, the kids put on their own concert to entertain their parents.

Other things which visitors of all ages can do include **boat trips**, deep-sea diving lessons, and there's even a chance to study local wildlife with the help of expert guides. If you're looking for a really original souvenir, then **there's also a group of artists working on the island. You can visit their studio and buy examples of their work.** If all you want is just a T-shirt or baseball cap, however, there are plenty of those for sale in the hotel giftshop.

Now, let's move on to the video...

page 75 PART 4

R: Look at the six statements for this part. You will hear a conversation between two teenage friends, Tom, a boy, and Sally, a girl. Decide if you think each statement is correct or incorrect. If you think it is correct, put a tick in the box under A for YES. If you think it is incorrect, put a tick in the box under B for NO.

Sally: Hello, Tom.

Tom: Hi... Listen, Sally, there's something I need to talk to you about. My mum says that if I want to go on that adventure weekend with the rest of the class, then I've got to raise the money myself.

Sally: Really? But why's she not going to pay for it?

Tom: Well, I guess it's because she had to buy all that extra sports equipment when I changed schools last year, and **it was rather expensive,** actually.

Sally: But **that wasn't your fault.** I mean, **everyone else's parents are paying.**

Tom: Anyway, I guess I'll have to get some work.

Sally: Work! You!

Tom: Alright, don't sound so surprised. I've worked before, you know.

Sally: You mean when you tried to set up that car-cleaning business.

Tom: **I know, I didn't make much money, but...**

Sally: ...my dad said his car was cleaner before you started!

Tom: **Alright,** but this time I thought we could put on a show. I'm sure we'd do well.

Sally: What do you mean 'we', and what sort of show?

Tom: A musical show, you know, with jokes and songs. **We could charge all the parents to come and see it,** and use the money to pay for the adventure weekend.

Sally: But just a minute, my parents are willing to pay for me, and so are everybody else's.

Tom: Oh, that's not the point. If we all raise the money ourselves, think what a good impression it will make. It'll be much easier to ask for other things in the future.

Sally: **I'm not so convinced about that.** They might just say, 'If you can raise the money for this, then you can do it for other things.'

Tom: But I was counting on you to play the guitar.

Sally: Have you told anyone else about this?

Tom: Not yet, but if you agree I'm sure the others will.

Sally: **umm... I'll let you know.**

Tom: Oh thanks, Sally.

Notes on the sample Speaking test

Practice Test 1 – Paper 3 Speaking

page 76

On the cassette, a sample Speaking test has been recorded. It comes between Practice Test 1 and Practice Test 2, which are both Listening tests. In the recording of the Speaking test, actors play the part of students. They perform the test tasks using PET-level language, but without mistakes of grammar, vocabulary or pronunciation.

Students should use the Speaking test on the tape to help them understand the best way to do the tasks. Remember, the examination tests the ability to speak spontaneously and to interact with another person. This means that it is not possible to learn what to say in advance. It is, however, a good idea to practise and be ready to perform the tasks in the best way.

On the tape, each part of the Speaking test is played separately. The students are using the materials in Practice Test 1 – Speaking on pages 76–8. Students preparing for the PET Speaking test should listen to each part of the tape, think about how the students do each task, and then attempt the same tasks themselves. They should not try to remember actual words, as they will need to give their own opinions and ideas. This will, however, be easier for them once they have heard a model.

For each task, a list of things to listen for is included below. Students can either work individually, or in pairs as a classroom activity. Students may need to listen to each part more than once. They should look at the visual material on pages 77–8 as they listen to Parts 2 and 3.

PART 1

In Part 1, students are told to ask each other questions.

Listen and notice:
- how many questions each student asks
- how long the answers are
- the different ways of asking
- how each student shows interest in what the other says.

Notice also:
- when a number is read out (remember, the number is on the answer sheet)
- when a word has to be spelt.

PART 2

In Part 2, students talk about the situation in the picture.

Listen and notice:
- how many times the instructions are given
- how the students begin
- how long each student speaks for
- how each student shows interest in what the other is saying
- how many of the pictures they talk about
- when they reach a decision.

PART 3

In Part 3, each student talks about a photograph.

Listen and notice:
- the topic of the photographs
- how each student begins
- the type of things they talk about
- what they do if they don't know a word.

PART 4

In Part 4, the students have a discussion on the same topic as Part 3, but giving their own opinions.

Listen and notice:
- the two things the students are asked to talk about
- how they begin
- how long each student speaks
- how each student shows interest in what the other is saying
- how they agree and disagree.

> **Note:** The Speaking tests in Ready for PET are sample tests only. They are not actual UCLES past papers.

Tapescript for Practice Test 2

Practice Test 2 – Paper 2 Listening

page 86 PART 1

RUBRIC = R

R: There are seven questions in this part. For each question there are four pictures and a short recording. For each question, look at the pictures and listen to the recording. Choose the correct picture and put a tick in the box below it.

Before we start, here is an example.

R: What's the time?
Man: Could you tell me the time please?
Woman: Of course. **It's twenty past four**.

R: The woman told the man the time. The second picture is correct and the tick has been put in box B below that picture.

Now we are ready to start. Here is a short recording for the first four pictures. Don't forget to put a tick in one of the boxes! Listen carefully…

R: One: What did the boy have for lunch today?

Mum: What did you get for lunch at school today?
Boy: Oh it wasn't bad really, there was even a choice. **I had chicken and chips**, but they also had pizza if you wanted it. Better than the tuna fish sandwiches we had yesterday. And they seem to have realized that people want a proper sweet afterwards, and so **there was a nice chocolate cake** instead of just the apples we've had before.

R: Two: Which programme will they watch on television?

Girl: What shall we watch on TV this evening?
Boy: There's football, a programme about elephants, a pop concert, or a film about mountain climbing. Which would you like to see?
Girl: Well, I certainly don't want to watch sport, and I've seen that film before. As you only seem to like classical music these days, **I suppose that leaves the wildlife**. What do you think?
Boy: That's fine for me.

R: Three: What time will the flight to Pisa leave?

Quickjet Airlines regret to announce a further 45-minute delay to flight QJ 35 to Pisa. **This flight is now scheduled to depart at 17.55 hours** from gate 25. Quickjet wish to apologize to passengers for the delay to their flight, which is due to operational reasons.

R: Four: Which activity did the girl do most of the time?

Boy: So, how was your holiday? Didn't you go to a place with all sorts of watersports?
Girl: It was great, actually. Although I did go swimming one day and there was a chance to do windsurfing if you wanted, it wasn't only watersports. **I spent almost all week mountain biking, in fact**, and I even got to try horse riding, but never again. I was terrified of falling off the whole time!

R: Five: Which is the missing handbag?

Hello, lost property office... yes... and where did you lose it?... I see... so, it's light-coloured leather, **with a long strap and a zip along the top...** Well, we've got a number like that. **Does it have a zip pocket on the side?... OK,** then I think I've got it here. When would you like to collect it?

R: Six: How will they travel this weekend?

Man: I think we should do something different this weekend. I'm bored with watching television. Why don't we get on a bus and go somewhere?
Woman: OK. I'm happy to have a change. How about hiring a motorbike and going down to the coast?
Man: **I'd rather hire a car.** With so much traffic on the road, I think motorbikes are dangerous.
Woman: OK, anything's better than that cycle ride we did last year. That was exhausting!

R: Seven: Which T-shirt do they decide to buy Sarah?

Boy: Which of these T-shirts shall we get Sarah for her birthday?
Girl: Well, she's got plenty of plain ones, so let's get one with a picture on it. Look, there's one here with kittens on it. That's nice.
Boy: Not for Sarah. She hates cats. But animals are a good idea. Horses, maybe... or... she loves going to the seaside, so how about this

one of a seabird? **Or even better, look, what about this one, with dolphins on it? Oh yes,** it's much better than the bird. **She'll love that.**

Girl:

page 87 PART 2

R: You will hear a woman talking about courses at a college. Put a tick in the correct box for each question.

Woman: Good evening. I've come to talk to you about courses at the Further Education College. Some courses are in the evening and some happen during the day. **They are all available to anybody over the age of sixteen.** Most courses are in practical subjects. In other words, we teach you, or show you, how to do things, so they're a good way of starting a new hobby. There are no examinations or certificates. These courses are meant to be just for fun.

To sign up for a course, you should come along to our Open Day on September the twentieth, or contact the secretary by phone. **You pay for your course month by month** and there's no deposit, so you don't have to pay anything before the course begins. After your first lesson, you decide whether you want to continue and if you do, you pay for the first month.

We are still offering our very successful foreign-language courses. Both beginner's and intermediate French and Italian are available again, and this year there will also be, for the first time, intermediate as well as beginner's Spanish, plus **a completely new course in beginner's Russian.**

Cookery courses are also popular. This year we're offering a range, from basic kitchen skills through to advanced cake-making, and courses on how to prepare meals for weddings and other large parties. **This year we're adding a course on vegetarian cookery** which I think will be very popular. Remember that on all cookery courses, students have to meet the cost of all the food items needed for the recipes.

Finally, many people asked us to include more courses on painting in our programme, and our teachers suggested other practical courses, like making pots, and so on. Although that would be interesting, **I'm afraid we don't have the equipment in the college at the moment.** There's a free room which could be used, however, and so it's a possibility for the future. Meanwhile, this year what we're doing is a new course in how to paint your own pots.

On the course, we provide white cups, saucers, plates, etc., and you learn how to paint designs on them. By the end of the course, you'll have your own hand-painted set to take home and use. **The course will run on Tuesdays and Thursdays** in the late afternoon, two hours each day, for the month of October only. If it's popular, another course could begin in the spring. The teacher is an expert in this type of work and I'm sure the course will be fun.

Now, if there are any questions...

page 87 PART 3

R: Look at the notes about an artist. Some information is missing. You will hear the artist talking about his work. For each question, fill in the missing information in the numbered spaces.

Artist: People often ask me why I decided to become an artist. Actually, it all started when I was a child. **I was eight years old** and I was getting better after one of those illnesses that children get. I felt alright, but I wasn't allowed to go out and I soon got very bored. I was given some paper and coloured pencils to play with and **I started drawing the birds I could see outside in the garden.** After that, drawing wildlife became my hobby and later I learnt how to paint, too.

My family was quite poor and, although they allowed me to study art, they weren't able to pay for my training. So when I was at college I started doing paintings of animals, especially **lions and tigers,** because I knew I could sell them to other students. I used the money I made to buy paints and other equipment.

When I finished college, I decided to make wildlife painting my career. To find customers, I held an exhibition of my work. **My father hired an empty furniture shop** in my home town and we filled it with my paintings. Fortunately, people liked my work and so we sold lots of paintings. I must say, although he doesn't know a great deal about art, **my father turned out to be a great**

salesman.

I also found that people like wildlife as much as I do, and they also like the way I paint. **I try to make the animals look as real as possible** and I try to paint them in their natural surroundings. People don't want to see pictures of animals looking sad in cages.

After that exhibition, there were articles about my work in the newspapers and my career had begun.

page 88 PART 4

R: Look at the six statements for this part. You will hear a conversation between two teenage friends, Jon, a boy, and Clare, a girl. Decide if you think each statement is correct or incorrect. If you think it is correct, put a tick in the box under A for YES. If you think it is incorrect, put a tick in the box under B for NO.

Jon: Hello, Clare. How was your holiday?
Clare: Oh, hi Jon. It was great, thanks.
Jon: **You'd never been abroad before, had you?**
Clare: **No,** it was alright though, **everybody there seemed to speak English,** so we didn't have too many problems.
Jon: Not like that place I went to last year. We really had to learn a few foreign words because nobody spoke English at all. If not, we'd never have got anything to eat in the restaurants.
Clare: Oh, where we went, all the menus were translated into English, so it was alright.
Jon: And was the food good?
Clare: OK. **We had lunch on the beach most days,** because my mum likes preparing picnics **and we all enjoyed that,** although it was boring getting all the stuff from the supermarket each morning. And then we had to eat out in restaurants in the evenings.
Jon: But didn't you like that?
Clare: Well, I just wanted to have burger and chips because that's my favourite, but my dad said we had to try the local food.
Jon: Well, **for me, trying all the foreign food is one of the best bits of going on holiday abroad.**
Clare: But I didn't know if liked it. Some of it was OK, but he made us try something new every evening. I wasn't allowed to have the same thing twice, even when I found something I liked.
Jon: **Oh, that's not fair! You should be allowed to choose what you want when you're on**

holiday. Holidays are meant to be about enjoying yourself.
Clare: That's right! That's what I said! Anyway, I did find some things I liked and **he let me have burger and chips on my last night there. Actually, it wasn't very nice** compared to what we have at home, so if we go back there again, I'll stick to the local stuff. Especially the fish, it was nice.
Jon: So your dad won in the end?
Clare: In a way.

Examples of student writing

In PET Writing Part 3, students are required to write a letter. (For more details, refer to page 37.)

A student can obtain a maximum of 10 marks for this letter: five for *task* and five for *language*. The mark for *task* reflects how well the student has succeeded in covering the three content points given in the instructions, and whether the message can be understood easily. The mark for *language* is based on the student's control of structure and vocabulary, and the range of language used. This includes correct spelling and punctuation, and the accurate and appropriate use of a variety of grammatical structures, as well as vocabulary relevant to the topic and linking words. Students at this level are not expected to produce writing which is completely free from errors. A mistake which does not prevent the writer from being understood is considered less serious than a mistake which interferes with communication. Students are given credit for being ambitious in attempting a range of different structures, even if they make some errors.

The following letters were all written by students attempting the Practice Tests on pages 72 and 85.

Note: as the first sentence of the student's letter is provided in the instructions, it is not included in the word count for each letter. Students are asked to write about 100 words.

Letters written for Practice Test 1 – Writing Part 3

1

> Dear Diana,
>   Thank you for the wonderful evening I had in your house. I had a great time with you, and your family is very kind.
>   I would like you come and spend an evening with me. I think it would be nice if I first cook the real Italian pasta for you. And then, if you will agree we can watch the video dance course I bought this morning. We will dance until we are too tired!
>   I would like you enjoy yourself, as much as I did round your house. It was really good fun making the cake and then letting your friend's eat some, it wasn't very nice was it?
>   Please let me know as soon as possible if you would like to come so I can organize the evening better.
> Lots of love
> Patrizia

Examiner's comment: very good
This student has completed the *task* very well. All three points in the instructions have been covered. The student has elaborated on plans for the evening at her house, and the thing she particularly enjoyed about the evening at her friend's house. In organizing her letter, this student has decided to talk about the first point in the instructions last. It is perfectly acceptable to do this (as long as the letter is coherent), although it is advisable to deal with the points in the order they are given in the instructions. The letter has a good closing sentence, even though the tone of it is a little formal. The student signs off with an appropriate phrase ('*Lots of love*') and a signature.

The student demonstrates good control of *language*. A range of tenses and structures is used, together with some complex sentence patterns and linking devices ('*first*', '*and then*', '*until*', '*as much as*', '*so*'). There are a few errors (eg '*like you come*', '*if you will agree*') but these do not impede communication. The phrasing of the invitation is completely appropriate ('*I would like you come and spend an evening with me*') and there is a good range of vocabulary relevant to the topic (eg '*great time*', '*kind*', '*cook*', '*watch*', '*dance*', '*enjoy yourself*' '*really good fun*'). The ideas in the letter are clearly organized into paragraphs.

2

> Dear Richard,
>   Thank you for the wonderful evening I had in your house. I enjoyed it really a lot expecially our water games in the swimming-pool.
>   I would like to have the recipe of the pankakes your mother baked.
>   It has been so funny when we made karaoke with your father and your mother asked him to cut it out!
>   It would be great if you could come to my house next week. You can catch the bus no. 978 and I will be at the bus station waiting for you. We can play basket in the park in front of my house, and then listen music or watch TV.
>   By the way, one thing is absolutely sure: I'm looking forward your visit.

Examiner's comment: good
This is a good attempt at the *task*. All three content points are covered fully, although the connection between the three things the writer particularly enjoyed is not made clear. There is an effective closing sentence, but the letter lacks a signing off phrase and a signature.

The writer shows fairly good control of *language*. The phrasing of the invitation is absolutely appropriate ('*It would be great if you could come to my house next week*'). A range of tenses and structures is used and there are only a few errors, which do not interfere with understanding. The letter could be improved if some linking devices were used to connect the three things the writer particularly enjoyed at the friend's house. At the moment, they are just a list. There is a fair range of appropriate topic vocabulary ('*water games*', '*recipe*', '*baked*', '*funny*', '*cut it out*', '*catch the bus*', '*watch TV*'). At the start of the letter, there are too many single-sentence paragraphs, but later on the writer attempts to organize ideas more clearly.

3

> Dear Mike,
>   Thank you for the wonderful evening I had in your house. Your parents are very nice and they have made me feel home. I had a very good time when we have played the computer and we loked the internet. But particularly I was very happy when we have played soccer with your friends in your garden. Now I want to invite you for a day for doing a lot of things together. If you accept the invite we could playing soccer in park or going with motorcycle ride in town. I hope that you'll come.
>   Antonio

Examiner's comment: adequate

This is a reasonable attempt to cover the *task*. The letter is a little short (85 words), and, although all three content points are covered, the third one is not dealt with fully. The ideas related to the third point are also not entirely relevant: the instructions ask for plans to spend '*an evening in your home*', not a day in the park or town. There is an appropriate closing sentence and signature.

This letter shows some control of *language*; the meaning is conveyed, but there are a number of errors, especially in the use of the present perfect, simple past tenses and prepositions. The way the invitation is phrased is grammatically flawed ('*Now I want to invite you for a day for doing a lot of things together*'), although the meaning is clear. Some simple linking devices are used ('*and*', '*when*', '*now*'), and there is some appropriate topic vocabulary ('*computer*', '*internet*', '*soccer*', '*motorcycle ride*'), but generally the language is unambitious. The letter could be improved if the ideas were organized in paragraphs.

4

> Dear Matt,
>   Thank you for the wonderful evening I had in your house. I enjoy this because we have played any songs with guiters and we have plei fotball, and we have eated a lot of pizza. For this, i went to invite you for the after seturday. We wil have lunch at Pizza's Way and after then we will met my frends and we will play basketball. See you Saturday, you must come!!
>   PJ

Examiner's comment: inadequate

Some attempt has been made to achieve the *task*, but it has not been done adequately. All three content points have been included but, because the letter is so short (62 words), they have not been dealt with fully. The plans related to the invitation are irrelevant, in that they refer to '*lunch*' and

activities outside the friend's home. An appropriate closing sentence and signature are included.

The student's control of *language* is erratic. The sentence structure is simple, but there are numerous basic errors, especially in tenses, verb forms and spelling. Some common words are spelt correctly in one place and incorrectly in another (eg '*play*'/'*plei*', '*will*'/'*wil*'). Students should check their work after they have written their letters, to correct simple mistakes for themselves. The wording of the invitation does not make clear what is intended ('*i went to invite you for the day after seturday*'). The range of vocabulary used is narrow.

Letters written for Practice Test 2 – Writing Part 3

5

> Dear Jill,
>   I want to tell you about my new English teacher. As he came into the class I immediately had the bad feeling he would make us working hard: he looks so severe, with those thik orrible glasses and his long beard, and he gave us the idea to be so proud that we sat down and no one dared to say a single word.
>   My classmates and I hope it's only the first impression and we keep saying that it won't be so bad as we begin getting to know each other better, but we miss the teacher we had last year.
>   I'm looking forward to hearing news about your first day at school and your impressions about your new teachers, hoping they're better than mine!
>   Love,
>   Daniela

Examiner's comment: very good

This student has completed the *task* very well. All three points in the instructions have been covered, and the description of the teacher deals with both his appearance and character. The students' feelings are also fully explained. The description of what happened in the class ('*we sat down and no one dared to say a single word*') is rather brief, but sufficient. There is an effective closing sentence.

This student uses *language* confidently and shows good control over it. There are some errors (eg '*make us working*') and spelling errors (eg '*thik orrible*'), but these do not impede communication. There is a good use of complex sentences, employing a range of tenses (present, past and future) and linking devices ('*as*', '*but*', '*and*' '*so proud... that*'), as well as appropriate topic vocabulary (eg '*bad feeling*', '*working hard*', '*severe*', '*thik glasses*'). The ideas are clearly organized in paragraphs.

6

> Dear Sandy,
>
> How are you? I hope fine. I had your new address from your cousin who live near my house. Thank you for your last letter. It was good to hear from you again. School started back up on the 14th – and it's boring as usual! This year there,s a new English Teacher in my class. At first, we supposed, she was dull and hot-tempered with us. Instead, after some days we spent with her, we found her amusing and cheerful. She's always ready to help pupils. Sometimes, we are inattentive during the lesson or we chat about this and that (especially girls) so teacher loses her temper but some minuts later she's again easy-going. She is also a pretty woman so boys (in my class) are very foll for the lesson! In short, we like it. What about you? I hope you had a good teacher too! I must stop now, my mother called me! Write soon. Bye for now.
>
> Yours
> Anna

Examiner's comment: good

This student makes a good attempt at the *task* but, as it is slightly flawed, would probably not achieve maximum marks. The student ignores the first sentence of the letter provided by the instructions and writes seven introductory sentences of her own. This means her letter is over long (162 words). Students are not penalized for writing more than 100 words, but can lose marks for digressing from the topic, as here. On the other hand, the student covers the content points well. The description of the teacher is good and the students' feelings about her can be inferred from this. These feelings are summed up by the sentence *'In short, we like it'*. This is an effective way of making sure that a content point has been dealt with satisfactorily. The second content point in the instructions (*'explain what happened in the class'*) has been slightly misunderstood; the student describes the teacher's lessons generally, rather than the *'last English lesson'* specifically, which may be penalized. Students should think hard about what the instructions are asking them to do before they start to write, and follow them exactly. The student ends her letter well.

This student uses language confidently and generally shows good control. There are some errors (eg *'live'*, *'there,s'*, *'minuts'*) but, except for one (*'are very foll for the lesson'*) these do not impede communication. She is ambitious in her use of complex sentences and uses a range or structures, tenses and linking devices (eg *'At first'*, *'after'*, *'or'*, *'so'*, *'some minuts later'*, *'also'*, *'In short'*), although one of these (*'Instead'*) is slightly inappropriate. She makes effective use of a wide range of appropriate vocabulary (eg *'boring'*, *'dull and hot-tempered'*, *'amusing and cheerful'*, *'inattentive'*, *'chat'*, *'loses her temper'*, *'easy-going'*). The letter would make an even better impression if it were divided into paragraphs.

7

> Dear Jane,
>
> I want to tell you about my new English teacher. We were waiting for our old teacher, when she came into the class: scary red hair and green eyes, matched with a yellow lemon dress. You can imagine what happened. We began to laugh and laughed the whole hour! And when she heard us, she began to scream and shout, her face became scarlat red! We really felt excited, she was so funny! But then, she ran out, closed the door, and we didn't see her anymore! What a pity, she was the best teacher we ever had!
>
> Write me soon!
> Tina

Examiner's comment: adequate

This student makes a reasonable attempt to deal with the *task*. All three content points are dealt with in a simple way, and only the second one (*'explain what happened in the class'*) is covered in any detail. The letter is also slightly short (92 words). The student could have given a more detailed description of the teacher or the students' feelings. The meaning is generally clear, although the reader may not be sure what is intended by the last sentence. Is it an attempt at irony? The letter closes appropriately.

The student's control of *language* is generally sound. A fair range of structures is used, with few errors, and there are some linking devices (*'when'*, *'then'*, *'and'*). Some of the language is very effective (*'scary red hair'*, *'You can imagine what happened'*, *'she began to scream and shout'*), though *'excited'* isn't appropriate in the context.

8

> Dear Elizabeth,
>
> I want to tell you about my new English teacher. He isn't as the other. His lessons aren't boaring.
>
> He is the youngest teacher of the school and in consequence is a very handsome man.
>
> For this reason all boys hate the new teacher while all girls are folling in love.
>
> Before I hated the English and I always had bad marks while now I love this sobjet.
>
> So now I hope to improve my English.
>
> Love,
> Katia

Examiner's comment: inadequate

This is an inadequate attempt at the *task*. There is some elaboration about the students' feelings for the teacher, which is good, but the description of him is very brief, and there is no mention of the second content point (*'what happened in class'*). The student signs off appropriately (*'Love, Katia'*) but ends the letter abruptly, without a friendly closing sentence. The letter is also far too short (68 words).

Because of the shortness of this letter, the student can't get a high mark for *language*.

Wordlist

Unit 1 Lesson 1
advice
block capitals
to collect
to complete (a form)
computer games
(to go) dancing
database
date of birth
details
driving
to enjoy
free time
hill walking
(to go) horse riding
instruction
to be interested (in
    s.thing)
interesting
Internet
keep-fit exercises
to play
notice
occupation
package
personal
shop assistant
to sign (your name)
signature
to spell
to study
suggestion
to surf (the Internet)
surname
warning
watersports
windsurfing

Unit 1 Lesson 2
armchair
to attend
books
to brush
climate
to comb
to deliver
desk
to dial
dishes
to dust
to feed
full name
furniture
(a pair of) glasses
hair
to hand in
international
interview
to invent
invention
to iron
to join in
make-up
medicine
meeting
mirror
to miss
mobile phone
nationality
pet
philosopher
to plug in
popular
to put away
to put on
to put up
questionnaire
radio
(an electric) razor
scientist
(a pair of) scissors
shirt
shoelaces
(a pair of) shoes
soap
(a pair of) socks
to suggest
to take off

teeth
to tidy
to tie
to turn on
to turn up
umbrella
walkman
washing machine
(to do the)
    washing-up

Unit 2 Lesson 1
blackboard
boring
cakes
CD (compact disc)
to check
to cook
correct
the cost (of s.thing)
document
(to send an) e-mail
enjoyable
equipment
favourite
to fry (an egg)
fun
to be good (at
    s.thing)
hobby
incorrect
ingredients
keyboard
to last
length
to look forward (to
    s.thing)
magazines
mouse
newspaper
screen
stuff
textbook
useful
video cassette
video player
videotape

Unit 2 Lesson 2
adult
adventure story
to advertise
amusing
to apologize
autobiography
to belong (to s.body)
biography
bookshop
to borrow
a bucketful (of s.thing)
to take care
charming
to create
cruel
damage
danger
daughter
deadly
delighted
demonstration
design
dinosaur
discover
to encourage
enemy
except
excitement
exciting
film star
to forgive
gossip
grandson
to guide
a handful (of s.thing)
heavy
hero
horror
humour

to hunt (for s.thing)
(a police) inspector
to investigate
to invite
journey
to lend
to look after
to look for
to manage (to do
    s.thing)
marvellous
to mend (s.thing)
a mouthful (of
    s.thing)
murder
mystery
opinion
to pass (time)
a plateful (of s.thing)
a pocketful (of
    s.thing)
powerful
to win
to prove
to publish
realistic
to recognize
to request
to respect
romance
science fiction
secret
shadow
to shoot
spaceship
space travel
a spoonful (of
    s.thing)
stage
to steal
stormy
successful
suitable
teenager
terrible
thriller
universe
victim

Unit 3 Lesson 1
accommodation
answerphone
arrangements
available
belongings
binoculars
booking
brochure
(to go) camping
campsite
credit card
destination
to discuss
downstairs
employee
excitement
excursion
experience
expert
facilities
first-aid kit
guest house
guidebook
handicrafts
hotel
luggage
map
market
minimum
mosquito net
nervous
nightlife
official
to pack
package holiday
passenger
photographs
(to have a) picnic

postcards
preparation
to prevent
to provide (s.thing for
    s.body)
to put up
receptionist
(to make a)
    reservation
to run out (of
    s.thing)
safari
scenery
shells
shower
sightseeing
souvenirs
(to go) sunbathing
(a pair of) sunglasses
suntan lotion
to supply
(to go) swimming
to take turns
tinned food
tour
training course
travel agency
trip
truck
unattended
value
variety
vegetables
vehicle
wallet
wildlife

Unit 3 Lesson 2
advertisement
application form
to apply (for a job)
architect
artist
bank clerk
biologist
businessman/woman
chemist
choice
colleague
to decide
decision
doctor
to earn (a salary)
to employ
employment
engineer
to fill in (a form)
fortunately
to get up
to govern
government
hard work
insurance
journalist
lawyer
lucky
manager
medicine
microscope
musician
(to go on) strike
to organize
physicist
police officer
profession
qualification
recording studio
responsible
to retire
retirement
shopping list
staff
stressful
to succeed
success
traffic
typical
unfamiliar

uniform
unsuitable
unusual
vegetarian
worried

Unit 4 Lesson 1
balcony
basement
bath
bathroom
bedroom
bedside table
blanket
blinds
block of flats
to blow-dry (hair)
calculator
chest of drawers
coffee table
cooker
curtains
cushions
dining room
dishwasher
dressing table
fridge
frying pan
garage
garden
hairdryer
hallway
kitchen
lamp
living room
mirror
packed lunch
pillows
to remember
seaside
shampoo
sheet
sink
sofa
stairs
storeroom
towel (rail)
wardrobe
washbasin
waterproof
windy
wood

Unit 4 Lesson 2
to advise
amount
amusing
anxious
attitude
attractive
bald
blond(e)
bored
boring
careful
careless
celebration
cheerful
to compare
to complain
confident
to correspond
curly
to develop
development
dull
education
fair
foolish
funny
hard-working
high school
honest
intelligence
lazy
to measure
middle-aged
miserable

pretty
professor
psychologist
to recommend
serious
shy
slim
smart
to smile
speed
strong
truthful
ugly
understanding
university
weak
wise
worried

Unit 5 Lesson 1
admission
to arrange
attraction
breakage
ceiling
changing rooms
to climb
collection
department store
discount
display
entrance (fee)
to exhibit
giftshop
gift-wrapping
to hire
home-made
in advance
to inform
interactive
items
leaflet
parcels
picture gallery
pleasant
plenty
to pre-book
public
reasonable
to receive
refreshments
representative
to reserve
ruin
sports centre
surrounding
to touch
traditional
view
weigh
well-known

Unit 5 Lesson 2
alternative
appointment
arrival
attendant
bank account
boarding pass
carriage
catch
to check in
to check out (of)
convenient
to cross out
to disturb
to draw out
driver
to pay (a fare)
to fill in (a form)
forename
furnished
gate
to get in
to get off
to get on
to give in
to hurry up

to land
license
luggage
meter
passenger
pilot
platform
position
report
station
stop
to switch on
to take off
ticket
timetable
tray table
to turn over
underground

Unit 6 Lesson 1
acceptance
arrangements
bargain
belt
boot
buttons
charge
cheque
clothing
collar
cotton
department
electrical
escalator
exotic
fashion
fashionable
goods
invitation
lift
out of order
pocket
receipt
receive
reduce
refusal
repair
sale
(a pair of) shoes
shopping centre
silk
skirt
sleeve
(a pair of) socks
speciality
spices
spots
stall
street market
stripes
sweater
tie
(a pair of) tights
tip
upstairs
vegetables
wallet
wool
zip

Unit 6 Lesson 2
advantage
convenient
crowded
dangerous
dirty
employment
entertainment
forest
fresh air
inconvenient
lonely
noisy
objects
peaceful
polluted
relaxing

rice
safe
spoon
stressful
sunny
traffic
transport
vehicle
way (of life)

Unit 7 Lesson 1
to add
bananas
beans
beef
burgers
butter
carrots
cheese
chicken
duck
fork
garlic
grapes
hard-boiled egg
herbs
impressive
knife
lamb
mayonnaise
to mix (together)
mixing bowl
mixture
mushrooms
olives
onions
oranges
owl
peas
pepper
plums
potato
to pour
recipe
salt
sausages
seeds
selection
sharp
snack
a spoonful (of
    s.thing)
steak
tasty
tomatoes
tomato sauce
triangle
tuna fish

Unit 7 Lesson 2
to afford
to allow
to annoy
argument
average
to blame
circumstances
cupboard
divide
dizzy
early
to expect
fancy
to find
to fit
fussy
knock
to lead to
likely
lucky
to mind
miserable
to operate
opinion
privacy
regret
relationship

to repair
to review
selfish
to separate
to share
shelf
storage
tidiness
to tidy up
wardrobe

Unit 8 Lesson 1
to appear
to attack
bat
to be born
bear
bee
to breathe
brilliant
to bury
changeable
cheerful
chicken
clear
clouds
coal
coast
cool
countryside
cow
damp
to defend
depressed
destroying
to dig up
to disappear
disease
to dry up
dull
dusty
elephant
encouraging
environment
extraordinary
extremely
eyesight
to fall down
fields
to fight
fine
to fly
foggy
forecast
freezing
frost
giraffe
gold
goldfish
gorilla
height
horse
human
hunger
inhabitants
iron
jump
kick
kitten
lightning
minerals
mist
monkey
mouse
nature
to overtake
owner
pavement
pet
to pick
pigeon
to pollute
to pour
poverty
to prevent
rabbit
rain

to reach
to realize
to rescue
rubbish
to set out
shark
shower
to slip
snake
snow
spider
to spoil
storms
to strike
to suffer
sunshine
to tear
thunder
tiger
tongue
urgent
warm
to watch
weather
to weigh
wind

Unit 8 Lesson 2
to admire
beach
bones
border
to break (down)
bush
camel
canal
canoe
cave
cliff
climb
continent
to cross
dense
desert
director
distance
district
eagle
edge
to emerge
expanse
fierce
to float
to flood
foreign
frontier
to hang
herd
hole
interval
irrigation
island
jungle
local
location
mountain
mud
nest
on foot
on horseback
passport
path
polar bear
primitive
to promise
to provide
to pull up
restful
rock
rope (bridge)
row
ruins
sand
satisfactory
scenery
shade
to shine

shore
to smell
soil
speed
stream
submarine
temperature
to tour
track
villain
waterfall
wave

Unit 9 Lesson 1
adventurer
to attend
balloon
baseball
to brush
circus
clown
crab
to discover
dolphin
driving test
entertainment
envelope
facts
to fail
to feed
flower
free-fall
frightened
golf
ground
gymnastics
hammer
handle
hockey
to introduce
to invent
judo
juggling
motor (boat)
nails
needle
net
notepaper
paint
pins
poetry
pot
to present
racket
refreshing
safety (rules)
sailing
scissors
seeds
skiing
skill
to slide
spade
stamp
table tennis
take up
training
tunnel
watering can
windsurfing
workshop

Unit 9 Lesson 2
accident
to ache
ambulance
aspirin
benefit
blood
to cure
deaf
deep
dentist
disease
documentary
to fall over
flu

Get well!
grateful
healthy
hearing (aid)
hospital
hurt
jogging
lifestyle
to look (after)
patient
sickness
sore throat
stress
survey
to take care (of)
toothache
unhealthy
valuable

Unit 10 Lesson 1
action (film)
actor
audience
backing (group)
camera
channel
characters
chat room
to clap
clubbing
to come up
comedian
commercial
crew
curtain
dancer
delicious
director
disc jockey
drummer
encore
film critic
interval
interviewer
lead (singer)
lines
performance
pianist
play
plot
pop group
to practise
presenter
programme
region
rehearsal
reviews
screen
series
singer
soap opera
(to be) sold out
soloist
stage
storyline
studio
violinist
website
wet

Unit 10 Lesson 2
communication
confused
to contact
face-to-face
fax
letters
misunderstanding
to pay attention
to phone
recent
relaxed
respect (for)
screen
skills
word-processing